The Turn of the

A Play

Ken Whitmore

Adapted from the story by
Henry James

Samuel French – London
New York – Sydney – Toronto – Hollywood

THE TURN OF THE SCREW

First presented at the Coliseum Theatre, Oldham, on 6th November, 1982, with the following cast:

Flora	Amanda Sutcliffe
Miss Grey	Denise Armon
Miles	Ian Lawson
Mrs Grose	Anne Rye
Mr Crimond	Alan Cody
Peter Quint	Alan Cody
Miss Jessel	Janet Amsbury

The play was directed by Pat Trueman

The action takes place in the sitting-room/hall of Bly, a large country house in Essex, and extends over a period of five months—from June to October, 1875

ACT I
PROLOGUE Shortly before dawn
SCENE 1 An afternoon in June
SCENE 2 An afternoon in July
SCENE 3 A morning in August
SCENE 4 3 a.m. on a September morning

ACT II
SCENE 1 An afternoon in October
SCENE 2 Two hours later—evening
SCENE 3 The next day. Late afternoon
SCENE 4 The next day. Late afternoon

CHARACTERS

Flora, aged 8
Miss Grey, 20
Miles, 10
Mrs Grose, 50
Mr Crimond, 35
Quint, 35
Miss Jessel, 28

The parts of Mr Crimond and Quint may be doubled

ACT I

The scene is the sitting-room/hall (known as the great hall) of Bly, a large country house in Essex. It is June, 1875

From the hall a staircase runs up L to a landing fronted by an oak balustrade. Two bedroom doors at least should be seen and the upper floors given an air of infinite spaciousness. On the ground floor are two doors on the right side of the hall and one door on the left. These lead R to the dining-room and little hall and L to the schoolroom. At the back facing the audience is a big bow-shaped window opening on to a terrace with steps leading down to parkland. The furniture is very fine and of the period and includes a desk, a chaise-longue, a sideboard, a low table and a grandfather clock. There is an oil lamp on the desk

PROLOGUE

The CURTAIN rises on the empty room in a pre-dawn gloom with the barest hint of light in the sky seen through the open-curtained window. There is a flicker of lightning, then a far-away grumble of thunder, then the window swings slowly open of its own volition. A man's figure, (Quint), is seen on the threshold. He moves slowly into the room, then turns his head to gaze towards the top of the stairs. Now a female figure, (Miss Jessel), is seen gliding down. She stops halfway and gazes at the man. He holds out his arms and she comes down and takes his hand. They walk out through the window and it slowly closes behind them. More lightning and thunder, then the Lights fade to a Black-out

SCENE 1

It is a brilliant sunny afternoon. The hall is empty

Flora is heard laughing and then she flings open the door from the little hall and runs in. She opens her arms in welcome to somebody in the little hall

Flora And this is the great hall. Come and see. Come — come.

Miss Grey enters and looks about in wonder. Miles comes in and takes her by the hand. Mrs Grose and Mr Crimond come in and stand watching at the door

(*Going to the window*) It's a lovely room. It fills up with sun. And there's the park and our old pony. And down there — ever so far — the lake where we go boating and have our picnics.

Miss Grey, hand in hand with Miles, goes to the window. Flora runs to the schoolroom door and opens it

And this is the schoolroom, Miss Grey. This is where you'll teach me tables and French and drawing. Come and see.

Miss Grey goes and looks in

The big geographical globe and the old piano. Miles plays the piano — don't you, Miles? — but I can't.

Miss Grey You never learned?

Flora No, I was too tired.

Miss Grey It's never too late. We must see if we can wake you up.

Flora (*taking Miss Grey's hand and leading her up the first stair*) Come on — I'll show you the bedrooms and our great dark tower. Come — come.

Crimond Flora, my dear.

Flora Yes, Uncle?

Crimond Don't run Miss Grey off her feet before she's even made up her mind to stay.

Flora (*to Miss Grey*) But you are staying, aren't you?

Mrs Grose Lord bless — we certainly hope so!

Crimond Mrs Grose, you're as bad as the children. Miss Grey mustn't be rushed and pushed. And Flora.

Flora Yes, Uncle?

Crimond How do you propose showing Miss Grey the tower when it's permanently locked and barred and sealed?

Miles Flora means we'll show Miss Grey the *staircase* leading to the tower. (*Pointing upstairs for Miss Grey's benefit*) It's just to the right up there — off the main landing.

Miss Grey (*amused*) This tower sounds highly mysterious.

Crimond The only mystery, my dear Miss Grey, is money. We had to close it off in the name of economy. (*Clapping to make the children move*) Now off you go, children, and don't detain our visitor more than five minutes. I must be off soon and Miss Grey and I have important matters to discuss.

Flora Yes, us!

And together with Miss Grey and Miles she goes off upstairs

Crimond Well — is she suitable?

Mrs Grose She's perfect. I only hope she finds *us* suitable.

Crimond Yes, she's the last scrape of a very deep barrel.

Mrs Grose The children have certainly taken to her.

Crimond Yes, and she to them, thank goodness. They're our best weapon, of course. Our young friend burns to be a little mother.

Mrs Grose You read the ladies like a book, sir.

Crimond It comes from long and concentrated study.

Mrs Grose Must you leave us so soon? Master Miles has only been home from school three or four hours and I know he's dying to have a talk with you.

Crimond Good Lord, is he? Sorry, I've an urgent engagement in town. (*He goes to the stairs and calls*) Miles — Flora!

Mrs Grose I don't believe that school suits him, sir.

Crimond Oh? Has the boy been belly-aching?

Mrs Grose Never, sir, he's a little gentleman in miniature. But he climbed out of that carriage this morning so pale and pinched. He was really down.

Crimond Then you must build him up. Bengers, Mrs Grose. Bengers.

Mrs Grose Yes, sir.

Crimond And what about Flora?

Mrs Grose Oh, happy as a lark, sir, as you've just seen with your own eyes.

Miss Grey and the children descend the stairs

Flora Miss Grey kept saying, "Is there more — is there more?" And Miles said, "We've only made a start — just wait till we go on a proper tour — you'll be amazed."

Crimond Yes, that's a thrill in store for the future, but now I must have the lady to myself for a moment. So shoo — off with the pair of you. Thank you, Mrs Grose.

Mrs Grose and the children go out to the little hall

(*To Miss Grey*) Well — and what do you make of Bly?

Miss Grey I can hardly say, sir. It's so big and beautiful. All those enormous empty rooms and long corridors and crooked staircases. It's like a castle out of a fairytale.

Crimond No, it's big and it's ugly and it's antique. But it is convenient, most of it. You might have noticed a few features of a building still older.

Miss Grey Of course.

Crimond Such as the tower. Quite useless, I'm afraid, but jolly picturesque.

Miss Grey But lovely! I had the strangest feeling as we wandered about the upper floors.

Crimond Do tell.

Miss Grey I felt the children and I were lost, like a handful of passengers in a great drifting ship.

Crimond Splendid! Because I'm offering you the helm.

Miss Grey I beg your pardon, sir?

Crimond I'm offering you supreme authority over this great ship and all who sail in her.

Miss Grey I? But surely Mrs Grose is in charge.

Crimond Mrs Grose is the first mate — the housekeeper. And there are plenty of other hands to help — cook — housemaid — dairywoman — old pony — old groom — old gardener. But the lady I appoint governess will command the ship. Well, how are your sea legs?

Miss Grey Sir, I'm barely twenty. This would be my first position. This morning I came up to London in a great flutter to answer your advertisement in the *Church Times*. And before I know where I am you whisk me to the depths of the countryside and propose placing me in charge of a great house.

Crimond (*amused*) The depths of the countryside? What — the wild and drear regions of nethermost Essex? Miss Grey, I detect in you a tremendous tendency to romanticize. No, don't be offended. I like it. And Bly will fit you like a glove.

Miss Grey But they're such serious duties. And this really is a place of very great loneliness, compared with what I've known.

Crimond (*glancing at his watch*) To become sordid for one moment, I offer twice the normal remuneration.

Miss Grey (*amazed*) I beg your pardon?

Crimond Twice the normal salary.

Miss Grey Twice? But why?

Crimond Great heavens, now I've alarmed you. To be plain: I like you — the children like you — Mrs Grose likes you. We throw ourselves on your sweet mercy. (*He takes her hand*)

Miss Grey (*pulling away*) Please, sir!

Crimond Miss Grey, you see before you a desperate man.

Miss Grey Desperate?

Crimond And that's an understatement. Two years ago my brother and his wife died in India — thank you, it was sad. And I woke up one morning to find myself the guardian of a small nephew and niece — I — a lone man without a jot of experience or a grain of patience. Well, Miss Grey, it's all been a tremendous worry and I've made a series of shocking blunders. You see, I pity the poor chicks most awfully, and of course I've done all I could. I sent then down here to my country place with the best people I could find to look after them. I even parted with my own servants to wait on them. Whenever I can I run down myself to see how they're faring. But the blessed thing is, you see, they have no other relations in the world and my own affairs take up all my time. In the beginning I had the luck to find an outstanding young lady to teach them, and all went swimmingly until — well — very sadly she went and died on us.

Miss Grey Oh, I am sorry.

Crimond Yes, and so are we. But that, of course, meant little Miles had to go off to school. And since then Mrs Grose has done all she can for Flora — in the way of manners and things — she's quite hopeless with the academic side. So you see, we really are in desperate need of — well — in a word — of you, Miss Grey. And so I throw myself at your feet. I'd be eternally grateful.

Pause

Miss Grey I can hardly refuse.

Crimond (*surprised*) You can't?

Miss Grey I fear not.

Crimond Miss Grey, I wish you a hundred years of life and a bag of gold. Now there's only one condition attached to this post.

Miss Grey A condition?

Crimond Just one – that you never get in touch with me.

Miss Grey But sir——

Crimond That you never trouble me – but never, never. You must neither appeal nor complain nor write to me about anything. You must meet all questions yourself, receive all moneys from my solicitor, and take the whole thing over and let me alone.

Miss Grey But, Mr Crimond——

Crimond Just yes or no. I must be off in one minute.

Miss Grey But, sir! (*She undergoes a great struggle, then sighs*) Very well. I agree to your condition.

Crimond Splendid! The bounty and the benison of heaven reward you. Now before I go, just promise me one thing.

Miss Grey What? There's more?

Crimond One final favour. Don't go. Stay here tonight.

Miss Grey Stay? But how can I? My belongings – my trunk – my clothes——

Crimond Can be sent up from Hampshire in a day – and your reverend father and your charming sisters acquainted with your new place in life at the same time. Until then Mrs Grose will provide all you need.

Miss Grey Well – I——

Crimond Good! It's done. Shake. (*He clasps her hand*) You know, it's been an education to meet you, but now I must fly. I've a pressing engagement in Harley Street. No, don't accompany me to the door. Mrs Grose will see me on my way. (*At the door of the little hall he remembers something, pats his pockets, and withdraws a sealed envelope*) I was forgetting. A letter from the lad's headmaster. Dreadful boring man. All chalk and sermons. I don't possess the patience to open it. (*Handing it over*) You open it. Read him – deal with him. But remember, not a word to me. It's all yours. Good-day, goodbye, good luck and thank you.

Crimond exits to the little hall

Miss Grey gazes after him in bewilderment and infatuation. Then she puts the letter on the desk, takes off her hat, and walks about touching the various treasures of which she is suddenly the custodian

Mrs Grose hurries in from the little hall, beaming

Mrs Grose Well, miss, so we have a new member of the family! Dear me, you don't know how happy and relieved I am!

Miss Grey Relieved? Why, is there something to fear?

Mrs Grose Fear, miss? No, miss. What makes you ask?

Miss Grey You speak as though I'd arrived at some Bluebeard's castle.

Mrs Grose Mercy! What an imagination! No, miss, it's just that having a pleasant young companion under these old rafters after all this time makes me the happiest woman the sun shines on, that's all. And the children are happy, too. They've taken a real fancy to you.

Miss Grey And I to them. They seem remarkable.

Mrs Grose Yes. Remarkable's the word. Most remarkable. Why, for good behaviour and sweetness and manners and consideration—you'll be carried away by them.

Miss Grey Yes, I'm carried away rather easily. I was carried away just now.

Mrs Grose By the master?

Miss Grey smiles and nods bashfully

Well, miss, you're not the first and I dare say you won't be the last.

Miss Grey Oh, I've no pretensions to being the only one.

Mrs Grose That's a good job.

Miss Grey (*gazing about*) This is all so amazing. I can't take it in. This morning I was the youngest sister of four at the parsonage. The baby. And now, all this. To manage the house—deal with the solicitor—open the letters—oh, there was a letter from the boy's headmaster. (*She takes up the letter from the desk and opens it*)

Miles appears at the balustrade on the landing and stands listening

But what can this mean?

Mrs Grose What is it, miss?

Miss Grey The child has been dismissed his school.

Mrs Grose But haven't they all been sent home?

Miss Grey Sent home? Yes, but only for the holidays. Miles may never go back at all.

Mrs Grose They won't take him?

Miss Grey They absolutely decline.

Mrs Grose But what has he done, the little precious?

Miss Grey offers the letter, but Mrs Grose puts her hands behind her back

I was never taught to read, miss.

Miss Grey Oh, I'm sorry. Do forgive me. Is the boy really so bad?

Mrs Grose Do the gentlemen say so?

Miss Grey (*after a glance at the letter*) They don't go into particulars. They simply say it would be impossible to keep him. And that can mean but one thing—that he's an injury to others.

Mrs Grose (*flaring up*) Master Miles? Him? An injury? Lord bless me. Why he's scarce ten years old. The dear faithful creature's as innocent as a pet dog. I tell you, miss, he's got all the virtues listed in the holy books—yes and a few more besides.

Miss Grey And you can honestly swear that you've never known him to be bad?

Pause

Mrs Grose Never? Oh, of course I don't pretend *that*.

Miss Grey You mean there have been occasions—?

Mrs Grose Oh, yes indeed, miss—thank God.

Miss Grey I see. You mean that a boy who never is bad——

Mrs Grose Is no boy for me. It wouldn't be natural.

Miss Grey I see. You like them with the spirit to be naughty? Well, so do I. (*She reflects*) But not to the point where they contaminate.

Mrs Grose Where they what?

Miss Grey Where they corrupt, Mrs Grose.

Mrs Grose (*laughing*) Corrupt? Master Miles? Why, miss, are you afraid he'll corrupt you?

And now they both laugh — rather hollowly

Miss Grey Tell me about the lady who was here before.

Mrs Grose The last governess? Well, *she* was young and pretty too. Almost as young and almost as pretty, miss, even as you.

Miss Grey I hope her youth and beauty helped her. He seems to like us young and pretty.

Mrs Grose Oh, he certainly did. It was the way he liked everybody. (*She stops herself*) I mean the master did — does — Mr Crimond.

Miss Grey But who were you speaking of before?

Mrs Grose Why, miss, of him.

Miss Grey The master?

Mrs Grose Yes, miss. Of who else, indeed?

Miss Grey Did *she* see anything in the boy that wasn't — quite nice?

Mrs Grose She never told me so, miss.

Miss Grey Was she careful — particular?

Mrs Grose Well, miss, she's gone. I don't like to tell tales.

Miss Grey I see. At least I think I do.

A pause

Flora joins Miles on the landing

Did she die here at Bly?

Mrs Grose (*increasingly uncomfortable*) No, miss, she went off.

Miss Grey Went off? To die?

No answer

She was taken ill, you mean, and went home?

Mrs Grose She was not taken ill, miss — not so far as I could see — not in this house. She left, miss, at the end of the year, to go home, as she said, for a short—— (*she stops*)

Miss Grey A short holiday?

Mrs Grose Yes, miss.

Miss Grey And then?

Mrs Grose She never came back. Just at the very moment I was expecting her . . .

Miss Grey Well?

Mrs Grose I heard from the master that she'd gone to glory.

Miss Grey But what did she die of?

Mrs Grose (*flaring up*) How should I know! By my life, miss, master never told me! (*Repenting*) I'm sorry, miss, but speaking of it upsets me. It was all

so sudden. Please, miss, I must get back to my work. I'm well behind today.
Begging your pardon, miss.

After an awkward curtsy, Mrs Grose hurries out to the little hall

Miss Grey, Miles and Flora gaze after her, as the Lights fade to a Black-out

SCENE 2

The same. It is towards dusk on a hot day

*Flora enters from the garden carrying a big bunch of flowers. She tries to cram
them into one vase, which is too small, then gives up and leaves the flowers on the
table. She looks to see if anybody is coming then starts tiptoeing upstairs*

*Miss Grey enters from the garden with a basket of flowers. She sees Flora going
upstairs and cries sharply*

Miss Grey Flora—not upstairs, darling.
Flora Why not?
Miss Grey I don't wish you to go up there, that's why.

Flora comes down. Miss Grey looks about for Miles

Miles? (*She goes to the stairs*) Miles, are you up there?
Flora He's still in the garden.
Miss Grey (*calling upstairs*) Miles—are you there? (*She starts to mount*)
Miles?

Miles enters from the garden

Miles Yes, Miss Grey?

Miss Grey turns

Miss Grey Thank heaven. (*She comes down and holds him with relief*)
Flora I told you he was in the garden.
Miss Grey Miles, promise me you won't go off on your own again like that.
Where have you been?
Miles I found a wasps' nest. I was just looking at the wasps going in and out.
Why?
Miss Grey Listen, both of you: I don't like you wandering off on your own—
especially when night's coming on.
Flora Why? Are there lions and tigers in the garden?
Miles No, but there are some terrible fierce tiger-lilies.

He and Flora laugh

Would you excuse me a moment, Miss Grey? (*He goes to the stairs*) I left
my book in my room.
Miss Grey No, Miles! Not up there.
Miles Beg pardon?

Miss Grey I don't wish you to go upstairs. Not at the moment.

Miles Could you tell me why not?

Miss Grey I'd like you to take these flowers to the kitchen and put them in water before they die. All right?

Miles Yes, of course. Come on, Flo, gather ye rosebuds while you may.

Miles and Flora gather up the flowers

Flora I do believe Miss Grey thinks there are lions and tigers *upstairs*.

Miss Grey Can you manage?

Miles Yes, fine. Would you mind opening the door?

Miss Grey (*opening the dining-room door*) And please tell Mrs Grose I'd like to see her right away.

Flora Yes, Miss Grey.

The children exit to the dining-room, leaving the flower-basket on the floor

Miss Grey goes to the window and closes it, then goes to the foot of the stairs and looks up, frowning

Mrs Grose enters from the dining-room

Mrs Grose Yes, miss?

Miss Grey Oh, Mrs Grose. I was just wondering – about the tower.

Mrs Grose Yes, miss?

Miss Grey Am I mistaken or is it kept locked at all times?

Mrs Grose Yes, miss, always. Why do you ask, miss?

Miss Grey At all times?

Mrs Grose Yes, miss – permanent – always.

Miss Grey You're quite sure?

Mrs Grose Well, I can only say it's never been open during my time here and that's close on fifteen years. What makes you ask?

Miss Grey holds her head for a moment

Is something wrong, miss?

Miss Grey No, I'm all right. I think I've been a little too long in the sun. Mrs Grose, how can you be so certain nobody uses the tower?

Mrs Grose Uses it? Whatever for?

Miss Grey Is there a key?

Mrs Grose A key to the tower?

Miss Grey Yes.

Mrs Grose As a matter of fact there is.

Miss Grey May I see it?

Mrs Grose You never intend going up there?

Miss Grey I'd like to see the key, that's all.

Mrs Grose goes to the desk, opens a bottom drawer and finds the key

Is that the one?

Mrs Grose Yes, miss.

Miss Grey Is it the only one?

Mrs Grose Yes, miss. Take a look at the rust. You can scrape it off with your nail. Can't have been used in years.

Miss Grey takes the key and examines it

Miss Grey It's just that when I was in the garden just now I happened to glance up and I saw a man standing on top of the tower.

Mrs Grose A man?

Miss Grey Yes.

Mrs Grose You couldn't have been mistaken?

Miss Grey You think I imagined it? A man staring down at me from the top of a tower?

Mrs Grose Staring?

Miss Grey Yes, as though I had no right to be there. As though the place belonged to him and I was an interloper. Even when he turned to go he was still staring at me.

Mrs Grose Where did he go?

Miss Grey He just turned away and — disappeared. (*She touches her head for a moment*) Or *did* I just imagine it? Some trick of the light . . .

Mrs Grose Have you perhaps a headache, miss?

Miss Grey No — yes — just a little one.

Mrs Grose (*helping her into a chair*) Better have a little sit down, miss. It's this weather. It's getting on top of all of us.

Miss Grey There can't actually have been a man, can there? Here's the key to prove it. Still, I might as well go up and make sure.

Mrs Grose No, miss!

Miss Grey Why not?

Mrs Grose I shouldn't venture up there, miss. They do say the staircase has crumbled away entirely. It was only a flimsy corkscrew thing twisting round the walls in the first place. And besides, look how dark it's getting. You wouldn't see a thing. You'd like as not break your neck. There was no man, miss. It was just a touch of the sun.

Miss Grey Yes, nothing a good night's sleep won't mend. If I can get one.

Mrs Grose You're not sleeping well?

Miss Grey It's just the strange little noises.

Mrs Grose Noises?

Miss Grey That the house makes, when it's settling down for the night.

Mrs Grose What sort of noises?

Miss Grey Oh, as if — I don't know — as if there were something astir.

Mrs Grose Something astir?

Miss Grey I suppose all old houses are the same. Once or twice I've imagined I could hear a child crying far away.

Mrs Grose Master Miles or Miss Flora. Having a little dream, bless them.

Miss Grey No, a child crying a long way off — like the wind in the trees. And I suppose that's exactly what it was. Combined with my over-active imagination. I've been rather on edge these last few days.

Mrs Grose Oh?

Miss Grey I've had some rather disturbing news from home. It unsettles one.

Mrs Grose Oh, dear, nothing serious, I hope?

Miss Grey Just little domestic troubles. But one worries, being so far away.

Mrs Grose Don't say you're thinking of leaving us, miss.

Miss Grey Good Lord, no.

Mrs Grose Thank heavens.

Miss Grey I really love Bly. I've never been so happy. You can't imagine the change from my life at home. I've got such freedom. Any woman would envy me. And the children are so alert, so responsive. They're almost too good to be true. And when they've gone off to bed and I take a turn in the grounds I get such a sense of—don't laugh at me, Mrs Grose, but I get a sense of *property*—almost as though I were *mistress* of Bly. (*Laughing at herself*) Yes, I feel as though my existence were justified at last—that by my great discretion and my quiet good sense I'm giving pleasure to the person who enticed me into coming here. Because that's what he did, you know.

Mrs Grose Mr Crimond?

Miss Grey Yes, he charmed me quite wickedly.

Mrs Grose Put you under his spell he did. I can see that.

Miss Grey I sometimes imagine, when I'm walking through the garden in the evening, that he'll suddenly appear and stand before me, and smile, and approve of all I'm doing here. That's all I'd ask. Just his approval. Nothing more.

Mrs Grose Oh, he'd be right proud of you, indeed he would. There's only one little point where he might have cause to differ.

Miss Grey Oh?

Mrs Grose I'm thinking of little Miles.

Miss Grey Miles? You mean about his school?

Mrs Grose Yes, miss, that horrible cruel charge.

Miss Grey But the charge is ludicrous. Miles cause trouble? You only have to look at him.

Mrs Grose I do, miss. I do nothing else. And I see nothing but goodness.

Miss Grey Because there's nothing else to see. His only crime is that he's too fine and fair for the nasty little school world and they've made him pay the price for it. They didn't want him there because he showed all the others up.

Mrs Grose So what do you mean to reply?

Miss Grey In answer to the headmaster? Nothing.

Mrs Grose And to his uncle?

Miss Grey Nothing.

Mrs Grose And to the boy himself?

Miss Grey (*magnificent*) Nothing.

Mrs Grose Then I'll stand by you, miss. We'll see it out together.

They shake hands

Miss Grey Together.

Mrs Grose Would it be too forward of me, miss, to——

Miss Grey To kiss me? Of course not.

They embrace

Oh, Mrs Grose, you do me so much good.

A rumble of thunder is heard

Mrs Grose Will you be all right now, if I leave you for a while?
Miss Grey I'll be fine.
Mrs Grose I'll see how my little darlings are doing with their flowers, bless them, and then give them supper and up to bed.

She exits through the dining-room door

Miss Grey picks up a letter from the desk and glances through it for the dozenth time. She examines a framed photograph of her family. She is upset. She sits down and starts writing a letter. Her attention wanders to the big rusty key. She picks it up, ponders, then goes to the stairs and starts to mount. At another rumble of thunder she stops, goes back to the desk and resumes her letter

Behind her at the window there is a flicker of lightning and Quint is staring in

Sensing his presence, Miss Grey puts down her pen, turns and gets up. They stare at one another for a long moment, then she rushes towards him but falls over the flower-basket on the floor

Quint disappears

She gets to her feet, opens the window and goes on to the terrace. When she is satisfied he is nowhere to be seen, she closes the window and stares in from the outside as he did

Mrs Grose, entering with a bowl of flowers, sees her face pressed against the window and screams and drops the bowl

Miss Grey comes in

Mrs Grose Lord bless me, miss! What's the matter? You startled the life out of me.
Miss Grey I've just seen him again.
Mrs Grose What?
Miss Grey That dreadful man—looking in—through that window.
Mrs Grose What? The same one?
Miss Grey The man on the tower.
Mrs Grose Then where is he now?
Miss Grey Goodness knows. I rushed out but he'd vanished like a——
Mrs Grose Vanished? What, again?
Miss Grey Mrs Grose, I'd like the truth from you about something, right away.
Mrs Grose Of course, miss. Would I tell you anything else?
Miss Grey Mrs Grose, is there some awful secret at Bly, about which nobody speaks?
Mrs Grose What do you mean, miss?

Miss Grey Is there some poor insane relative kept in confinement here? Locked up in that tower?

Mrs Grose Mercy! No!

Miss Grey One who sometimes breaks free and prowls and hovers about?

Mrs Grose Prowls and hovers? God help us. No, miss, I swear.

Miss Grey Then who was it? Who is he? What does he want?

Mrs Grose Lord knows, miss. Was he a gentleman?

Miss Grey No. No!

Mrs Grose Nobody from about the house? Nobody from the village?

Miss Grey I've never set eyes on him.

Mrs Grose How long was he standing there?

Miss Grey Until I went out to meet him.

Mrs Grose Merciful powers! I couldn't have gone out.

Miss Grey Neither could I. But I did. I have my duty. I have to protect the children.

Mrs Grose What did he look like?

Miss Grey Like nobody.

Mrs Grose Nobody.

Miss Grey You want a description? All right, he wore no hat. He had red hair, very red. Good straight features. Yes, and red side whiskers. His complexion was pale, yes, unnaturally white, as white as paper. And there was something else. (*She thinks*) Yes, a birthmark. A small round birthmark on his right cheek.

Mrs. Grose (*sharply*) A birthmark?

Miss Grey Yes — about the size of a farthing. And his eyes were sharp and very strange. Rather small and fixed. Staring eyes. And his mouth was wide and thin. Of one thing I'm certain. He wasn't a gentleman.

Mrs Grose A gentleman? What? *Him* a gentleman? That was the last thing you'd call him.

Miss Grey What? You know him?

Mrs Grose Handsome? Would you call him handsome?

Miss Grey Very.

Mrs Grose And his clothes?

Miss Grey Somebody else's. They were smart but they didn't belong to him.

Mrs Grose No, they belonged to the master.

Miss Grey Mr Crimond? But you mean you do know him?

Mrs Grose Quint.

Miss Grey Quint?

Mrs Grose Peter Quint. Mr Crimond's own man. His valet when he was here.

Miss Grey When Mr Crimond was here?

Mrs Grose He never wore the master's hat, but he did wear — well, there were waistcoats missed. Both him and the master were here last year. Then the master went away and Quint was left alone.

Miss Grey What do you mean, alone?

Mrs Grose Alone with us. In charge.

Miss Grey A valet in charge? (*She pauses*) But what became of him?

Mrs Grose Mr Quint went too.

Miss Grey Went where?

Mrs Grose God knows where. He died.

Miss Grey Died? But how?

Mrs Grose He was found, miss, one winter's morning. Found by a farmhand going to work.

Miss Grey Found?

Mrs Grose Stone dead, miss, on the road to the village. He'd been at the public house the night before, drinking more than was good for him.

Miss Grey Drunk, you mean?

Mrs Grose So they say, miss. They found his body at the bottom of a steep icy slope. It seemed that in the dark he'd taken the wrong path altogether. There was a great deep wound to his head.

Miss Grey From the fall?

Mrs Grose So it seems.

Miss Grey What did they bring in — at the inquest?

Mrs Grose Well, the icy slope, the turn mistaken in the dark, the drink he'd taken . . .

Miss Grey Accident? They brought it in as an accident?

Mrs Grose That's what they called it.

Miss Grey But you think — ?

Mrs Grose It's not my place to think, miss. But there was a lot of chatter in the village.

Miss Grey Why, what was there to chatter about?

Mrs Grose Because the man was naught but a villain — a devil. Because there were things about him that would have accounted for a deal more than a mere slip on the ice.

Miss Grey A villain? A devil? I don't understand.

Mrs Grose It's the truth, miss.

Miss Grey And yet he was placed in charge of these two innocent children? What on earth were you all dreaming of?

Mrs Grose It was the wish of the master.

Miss Grey But wait. Why are we talking about Quint? How could Quint be the man at the window if he's dead?

Mrs Grose No, miss, it was just the way you described him — the red hair and the birthmark. But of course, it's not possible. The man's cold in his grave.

Miss Grey Then who was it?

They stare at one another as the Lights fade to a Black-out

SCENE 3

The same. Morning, a few weeks later

Before the Lights come up Miles is heard playing the piano in the schoolroom. The Lights come up. Flora sits painting at an easel by the window

Mrs Grose comes quietly in from the little hall with a letter on a salver and stands listening to the music and watching Flora

Flora continues painting for a while and then speaks without turning

Flora Good-morning, Mrs Grose. What are you doing?
Mrs Grose Why, Miss Flora, you've got eyes in the back of your head. An enchanted child, that's what you are.
Flora Why were you just standing there?
Mrs Grose I was just saying to myself there never were two nicer children in this sad old world. Nor such clever ones. Just listen to Miles playing his little heart out. Is Miss Grey in there with him?
Flora Yes.
Mrs Grose Is she a good music teacher?
Flora Better ask Miles. I'm no judge.
Mrs Grose Well he certainly sounds better to me. (*Looking over Flora's shoulder*) And whoever saw such a beautiful painting by a girl so young?
Flora It's all right.
Mrs Grose All right? You've got every reflection in that lake and the trees look so real you expect to see a bird fly up. (*Suddenly she sees something*) Miss Flora?
Flora Yes?
Mrs Grose That man — what's he doing there?
Flora Which man?
Mrs Grose There — why, that man you've painted — hiding between the trees on the edge of the lake.
Flora A man? That's just the old pine tree that was split by lightning last month.
Mrs Grose Which pine tree?
Flora Just look out of the window and you'll see it.
Mrs Grose (*looking out*) Why, Lord bless, so it is. Nothing but an old tree.
Flora Is that a letter for Miss Grey?
Mrs Grose Yes, dear.
Flora From home?
Mrs Grose Now then, Miss Flora, it's not ladylike to ask where people's letters come from. We have to respect their privacy.
Flora They make her sad, don't they?
Mrs Grose What makes you say that?
Flora She's never happy when the post's been.
Mrs Grose Well, is she keeping you happy, that's what counts?
Flora Oh, yes, I'm all right. Miles gets a bit fed up, though. He wants to go back to school.
Mrs Grose Does he, indeed? Well, we'll have to wait and see.

The schoolroom door opens and Miss Grey comes out and talks to Miles inside

Miss Grey Just take it a little more slowly and try to get plenty of feeling into it. (*She sees Mrs Grose*) Oh, Mrs Grose, is that for me?
Mrs Grose Yes, miss.

Miss Grey's face falls. She glances at the letter and puts it in her pocket, then looks over Flora's shoulder

Miss Grey Flora, that's exceptionally good.
Mrs Grose And it isn't a man, miss, if that's what you were thinking.
Miss Grey A man?
Mrs Grose In the picture. It's just an old tree stump.

Miss Grey studies the picture more closely, then looks out of the window

Miss Grey Yes, of course it's a tree. It was struck by lightning a few weeks ago. Now, Flora, I think it's time you went in to your brother and did some singing practice.
Flora Oh, Miss Grey, please.
Mrs Grose Run along, my cherub. Miss Grey wants to read her letter — and I'll be going, too, miss.
Miss Grey No, stay, Mrs Grose. I've something to say to you. Well, Flora, off you go.

Flora goes into the schoolroom, leaving the door ajar

Miss Grey starts to say something, but can't

Mrs Grose Is there anything amiss?
Miss Grey I'm not sure. It's all so very curious. I mean that you should see a man, where no man existed.
Mrs Grose What? Oh, the picture. But it wasn't a man at all, miss — just a tree.
Miss Grey Yes, it's just a tree. The strange thing is that down by the lake this afternoon, when the children and I were having our picnic——
Mrs Grose Yes, miss?
Miss Grey I was nearly sure — no, I was certain — there was a man hiding among the trees.
Mrs Grose What?
Miss Grey Yes, a man. Watching us.
Mrs Grose You don't mean —? Not him?
Miss Grey Yes. And I'm almost certain he was looking for someone.
Mrs Grose You mean Quint?
Miss Grey The man I saw before. On the tower. At the window.
Mrs Grose And he was looking? Looking for you?
Miss Grey No, he was looking for Miles.
Mrs Grose Miles? How do you know?
Miss Grey I just know, I know, I know. And so do you know, Mrs Grose.

Mrs Grose goes and closes the schoolroom door before returning to Miss Grey. The piano music stops shortly

Mrs Grose But, miss — what if the boy should see him?
Miss Grey That's exactly what he wants.
Mrs Grose Master Miles — wants to see Quint?

Miss Grey No, heaven forbid. The man. He wants to appear to them. But he won't. I won't let him.

Mrs Grose Miss, if this is true, how can you stop him? I mean, if he's——

Miss Grey If he's diabolical? If he's returned from the dead?

Mrs Grose Merciful powers, miss, don't even say such things.

Miss Grey We must say them. We must face them. Dear Mrs Grose, try, try to understand. You could easily suspect me of something like madness, I know, and I wouldn't blame you. But I've a great sensitivity to such impressions, and I'm certain that man is going to appear again. But he won't appear to those children, I promise you, no, never, because I will be a screen. I'll stand before them and the more I see, the less they will. Why else am I here if not to shelter them? They've got no-one but me in the world, and all I have — well, I have them. I've been singled out, Mrs Grose, for an exceptionally dangerous task. I see that now. It's going to call for strong nerve, but there'll be something fine in letting it be seen, in the right quarter, that I can succeed where any other girl on earth would — I'm sorry. You must think I'm rather queer company. Almost as queer as the company I receive.

Mrs Grose No, miss.

Miss Grey No? You mean you believe me? You don't think I might be — a little odd?

Mrs Grose No, miss.

Miss Grey Thank God.

Mrs Grose Why, you described the man to the life. You described his clothes, his hair, the very whiskers on his chin. How could I doubt you?

Miss Grey Thank you, Mrs Grose. So we can face this out together?

Mrs Grose We must. We've been given no choice. We must lean on each other and bear it out for the sake of those innocent children.

Miss Grey Mrs Grose, have you ever noticed — they never speak of him?

Mrs Grose Of Quint?

Miss Grey About the time they spent with him, his name, his history, nothing.

Miss Grey The little lady won't remember. She never heard or knew——

Miss Grey How he died? Perhaps not. But Miles would remember.

Mrs Grose Please, miss, don't mention it to the lad.

Miss Grey Still, isn't it singular?

Mrs Grose That the boy's never spoken of him?

Miss Grey Never by the slightest allusion. Yet you say Miles and he were such great friends.

Mrs Grose Friends? Lord bless me, not at all. Why, the very idea. It was just Quint's own fancy — to play with him — to spoil him. Quint was much too free.

Miss Grey Too free? With my boy?

Mrs Grose With everyone.

Miss Grey And he was definitely wicked?

Mrs Grose Miss, upon my soul, I'd rather be hugged by a snake.

Miss Grey Yet you said nothing of his wickedness to Mr Crimond.

Mrs Grose Tale-bearing? The master couldn't abide it. He was terribly short with anything like that, and as long as people were all right to him, well——

Miss Grey But good heavens, woman, even so, he should have been told.

Mrs Grose Yes, I dare say I was wrong, but I was frightened.

Miss Grey Frightened of what?

Mrs Grose Of the things that man could do.

Miss Grey But not frightened of his influence on precious innocent lives? They were in your care, Mrs Grose.

Mrs Grose No. Would to God they had been. The master believed in Quint and placed him here because he was supposed to be unwell and the country air so good for him. So Quint had everything to say—yes, even about the children.

Miss Grey That creature—everything to say about them? And you could stand by calmly and bear it?

Mrs Grose Not calmly. No. I couldn't—and I can't now.

Miss Grey (*hearing something*) Mrs Grose—listen—be quiet for a moment.

Mrs Grose What is it?

Miss Grey The children. So quiet. Not a sound. Oh, no, why did I let them out of my sight? (*She hurries to the schoolroom and opens the door*) Are you all right? Why aren't you singing? You'd better come in here for a while. You've had enough practice for one day. All right, Mrs Grose, thank you, that will be all.

Mrs Grose Thank you, miss.

Mrs Grose exits to the little hall

Miles and Flora come in. Miles goes to inspect his sister's painting

Flora Miles was being rude about my singing. I wish you'd tell him off.

Miss Grey Rude? In what way?

Miles I said she was like a strangled peahen. I'm sorry, I take it back. Florence, you sang like a nightingale.

Miss Grey There, that's a handsome apology.

Miles Yes, a strangled nightingale.

They all laugh

Still, you can paint a picture, Flo. Better than you can sing a song. Thank goodness.

Miss Grey That's quite enough, Miles. A gentleman doesn't insult a lady even in fun. Now play with your jigsaw puzzle for a few minutes while I read my letter.

Miles (*sympathetically*) Letter from home?

Miss Grey Yes, Miles.

Miles Hope the family's all right.

Miss Grey Thank you, Miles.

Miss Grey sits and reads. Miles and Flora spread the jigsaw pieces on the carpet and sit facing the stairs. Miss Grey reads her letter and from her expression it seems a worrying one. Suddenly *she looks up*

   A figure has appeared on the stairs, Miss Jessel, a woman in black, pale and dreadful, with eyes devouring Flora

Miss Grey starts to rise, but changes her mind and subsides, studying the children's reaction. As though by accident, Miles and Flora turn until their backs are to Miss Jessel

   Miss Jessel disappears

Miss Grey rises with hard-won composure and pulls the bell-rope

Miss Grey Put that away, now. I think it's time for a little more music practice.
Flora Oh, Miss Grey, we've only just started.
Miss Grey Put the puzzle away, please, and do as you're told.
Miles Come on, Flo. We can do it later. (*To Miss Grey*) Was it bad news? Are your people all right?
Miss Grey Thank you, Miles, they're perfectly fine.

Mrs Grose enters from the little hall

She looks questioningly at Miss Grey who gestures her to be silent until the children have gone. Miles puts the box of jigsaw pieces on the table and stands thoughtfully at the schoolroom door

Flora I don't really sing like a peahen, do I?
Miss Grey No, Flora, of course not.
Miles Not exactly. Come on, Flo.

He politely holds the schoolroom door for Flora, and they both exit

Miss Grey again has difficulty broaching a subject with Mrs Grose

Mrs Grose Yes, miss?
Miss Grey Mrs Grose, this house——
Mrs Grose Yes, miss?
Miss Grey This house is swarming with ghosts. And the children know. It's horrible. They know.
Mrs Grose They know what, miss?
Miss Grey All that we know. And God knows what else besides. Not five minutes ago in this room, they saw.
Mrs Grose Saw? What, they told you they did?
Miss Grey Oh, not them. Don't you see? That's the horror. They kept it to themselves, or thought they did. A child of eight—a child of ten.
Mrs Grose But miss, how do you know they saw, if they kept it to themselves?
Miss Grey I was here. I saw with my eyes. They were perfectly aware.
Mrs Grose Of him, you mean?
Miss Grey No, Mrs Grose. Of her.

Mrs Grose What? A woman?

Miss Grey A woman in black. A pale and dreadful woman — and such a face. The children sat there — on that carpet — playing with their puzzle. And in the midst of it she came.

Mrs Grose Came how? From where?

Miss Grey From where they come from! She suddenly appeared on the stairs and stood there.

Mrs Grose And have you seen her before?

Miss Grey Never. But the children have, and so have you.

Mrs Grose Me? But who on earth——?

Miss Grey The last governess. The one who died.

Mrs Grose Miss Jessel?

Miss Grey Miss Jessel. (*She pauses*) All right, tell me I'm mad.

Mrs Grose No, miss, by no means. Only how can you be sure?

Miss Grey Very well! Ask Miles and Flora. They're sure. No, leave them alone. They'll swear they saw nothing. They'll just lie.

Mrs Grose Lie? Those babies? Oh, to spare you, you mean.

Miss Grey To spare me? (*She laughs*) No, there are depths here, Mrs Grose, terrible depths. The more I go over it the more I see and the more I see the more frightened it makes me.

Mrs Grose You're frightened of seeing her again?

Miss Grey Oh, no, that's nothing now. Nothing. I'm frightened of not seeing her. That she'll come again and I won't be aware of it, but that Flora will.

Mrs Grose Flora? But why Miss Flora?

Miss Grey Don't you see? It's Flora she's after. Her eyes never left the child's face. They were drinking her in.

Mrs Grose But what could she want with the child?

Miss Grey To get hold of her. And Flora knows it. She knows it and she doesn't care. In fact I believe Flora rejoices in it.

Pause

Mrs Grose The woman was in black, you say?

Miss Grey She was in mourning.

Mrs Grose But striking to look at? A beauty?

Miss Grey Oh, handsome, wonderfully handsome; but wicked, Mrs Grose; a horror of horrors.

Mrs Grose She was wicked. The pair of them were wicked.

Miss Grey And what was there between them?

Mrs Grose There was everything.

Miss Grey Everything? What? In spite of the difference of their rank?

Mrs Grose Everything. Can you imagine it? She such a lady and he so dreadfully below.

Miss Grey The man was a hound.

Mrs Grose Well I've never seen one like him. He did exactly as he pleased.

Miss Grey With her? It must have been what she wished, too.

Mrs Grose But she paid for it, the poor creature.

Miss Grey By her death? So you do know how she died.

Mrs Grose No, miss, I know nothing. I only know that she had to leave us in
  a great hurry.
Miss Grey But why?
Mrs Grose Well, miss, she couldn't have stayed. Not in that condition.
Miss Grey In what —? Oh — I think I see.
Mrs Grose Yes, miss. In no condition for a single lady to find herself in and
  still keep her reputation.
Miss Grey I see.
Mrs Grose Fancy it, miss. A governess.
Miss Grey And this was the pair who were entrusted with the lives of those
  two infants? My God, I think we're too late. Can't you imagine what those
  children must have seen and heard? Mrs Grose, they've got to be saved, but
  I don't do it. I don't shield them. But I will. I'll watch every hour of the day,
  every minute of the night. I won't rest, I won't sleep. But I think it's too
  late. I think they're already lost.

*Flora is heard singing "Nymphs and Shepherds", off, as the Lights fade to a
Black-out*

SCENE 4

The same. It is three in the morning

*The room is dimly lit by an oil lamp and a candle. Miss Grey lies motionless on
the chaise-longue covered by a blanket. A book she has been reading is on the
floor nearby*

*A figure with a candle passes along the landing, pauses at the top of the stairs,
then glides down and crosses to Miss Grey. It is Mrs Grose in nightcap, gown
and shawl. She bends over the sleeper*

Mrs Grose Miss Grey? Do you hear? (*She picks up the book and drops it on
  the table in an effort to tidy up and wake up at one and the same time, but this
  fails to wake Miss Grey, and Mrs Grose tries again*) Miss Grey, it's three in
  the morning. (*She touches Miss Grey's dangling hand, with no response, then
  takes her by the shoulders*)

Miss Grey jumps up and both women cry out

Miss Grey No! Don't do it! (*And then she sees who it is*) Mrs Grose — oh,
  thank heavens.
Mrs Grose Miss, what a fright you gave me.

Miss Grey gets up and cloaks herself in the blanket

Miss Grey Is anything the matter? What time is it?
Mrs Grose It's gone three, miss, and you should have been in your bed long
  ago. You haven't given yourself a good night's rest for ages and ages and
  it's doing you no good.
Miss Grey I'm all right. Don't worry about me.

Mrs Grose Stay there and I'll make you a nice mug of Bengers; it'll steady your nerves; they're at snapping point, indeed they are.

Miss Grey No, one moment. What brought you down? Did you hear something?

Mrs Grose Lord, miss, no, it's just that you've got me restless, too.

Miss Grey What? So you sense it as well?

Mrs Grose All I sense is you lying down here night after night making yourself tired and irritable.

Miss Grey Something must have woken you.

Mrs Grose Your book falling on the floor very likely. Any little noise in this place at night echoes like a gun going off.

Miss Grey So you did hear something.

Mrs Grose Miss, don't make so much of every little thing. There's been nothing amiss at all for a long while, and you've said it yourself. Just try to relax and enjoy yourself.

Miss Grey Relax? That's just what they're waiting for.

Mrs Grose Miss, they've gone. If ever—— (*She stops herself*)

Miss Grey You mean if ever they came in the first place? If they weren't just a figment of my luxuriant fancy?

Mrs Grose I never said such a thing. But now it's all over. The children have showed no sign, have they?

Miss Grey Oh, nothing. Nothing but that same unnatural goodness.

Mrs Grose Unnatural? How can goodness be unnatural?

Miss Grey It's a goodness that's too perfect to be true.

Mrs Grose Miss, honestly, you try my patience. If the children are good then thank the Lord and ask no questions.

Miss Grey But what's behind it? Children are natural anarchists. I was one myself the day before yesterday. But these two are like impossible paragons in some manual of model behaviour.

Mrs Grose But they're so fond of you.

Miss Grey Too fond.

Mrs Grose Too fond? Too good? Come, miss.

Miss Grey They've never wanted to do so much for me. I don't mean just learning their lessons better and better, which they do. No, I mean devising all manner of treats to surprise me, to delight me. And they succeed. They really do carry me away. Who could resist? They read me passages from books. They tell me stories. They act my charades. They pounce out at me in disguise — as animals — as characters from history — tigers and Romans and Shakespeares. They learn enormous poems by heart and recite them so beautifully, reams and reams, little miracles of memory. The moment I came here I knew they were unusual, that they had a wonderful facility for knowledge, that they'd be a joy to teach. But the flights they're making now are extraordinary, especially Miles. So much knowledge accompanied by such perfect behaviour. And yet stop and think, Mrs Grose.

Mrs Grose Think, miss?

Miss Grey Yes, just think. Why should such a paragon be removed from his school? Why?

Mrs Grose Jealousy, miss. You said it yourself. Wicked jealousy and spite at his wonderful goodness.

Miss Grey His wonderful goodness. We keep coming back to that, don't we? That's the only side he's shown me. But not you. Not always. You've seen a dark side of Miles.

Mrs Grose Me? A dark side?

Miss Grey Oh yes, you have. You told me once he hadn't always been perfect. And by way of excusing him you said a boy who was always good wouldn't be a boy for you. What were you referring to, Mrs Grose? What had he done that lapsed from perfection for a moment?

Mrs Grose I can't call any such occasion to mind.

Miss Grey Oh, come.

Mrs Grose Well . . . there was just one occasion when I had cause to be cross.

Miss Grey Yes?

Mrs Grose It was the time I ventured to point out to him that he was spending too much time with Quint.

Miss Grey Miles spent too much time with Quint?

Mrs Grose They were never out of each other's company. In the end I spoke to Miss Jessel about it.

Miss Grey And?

Mrs Grose I've never seen such a temper. I thought she would hit me. And after that she was as chill as an icicle with me. But I wasn't going to let her beat me and I went straight to Master Miles himself and told him, in no uncertain manner that I liked to see young gentlemen not forget their station. I said Quint was nothing but a menial, and that's when he took my breath away. He just came straight back and said so was I.

Miss Grey And you forgave him that?

Mrs Grose Wouldn't you, miss?

Miss Grey No. Yes, I suppose I would. But what else? There must be more. How else was Miles bad?

Mrs Grose He denied things.

Miss Grey What things?

Mrs Grose He denied they'd been going everywhere together — with Quint lording it as though he was the tutor and Miss Jessel only responsible for the little girl.

Miss Grey I see. So you mean while the boy was with the man——?

Mrs Grose Yes, Miss Flora was with the woman. It suited them all very nicely.

Miss Grey But Miles denied all this? He lied?

Mrs Grose I wouldn't say he lied. After all, Miss Jessel didn't mind. She didn't forbid him.

Miss Grey And Miles used that as a justification?

Mrs Grose He never mentioned her. Not in connection with Quint.

Miss Grey You mean he tried to hide what was going on between them?

Mrs Grose He didn't say anything. He denied — he denied.

Miss Grey He denied so much that it became obvious that the pair were up to no good? And that he was fully aware of it?

Mrs Grose I don't know — I don't know! Please, let me make you a nice hot drink. It's freezing down here.

Miss Grey But you do know, Mrs Grose. You know he was deliberately hiding what that awful pair were doing together.

Mrs Grose He couldn't hide it!

Miss Grey But he tried. Admit that he tried.

Mrs Grose All right — he tried!

Miss Grey There. At last. He tried. Tried to cover their disgusting relations. Think what it means. How they must have twisted him, corrupted him. What they must have made of him.

Mrs Grose Oh, miss, nothing that isn't nice now!

Miss Grey Nice? Oh yes. Nice to us. Nice to our face. But at school a fiend, apparently.

Mrs Grose That's not true, miss!

Miss Grey Yes, Mrs Grose, an angel in the home but such a devil at school that he has to be removed before he corrupts the others. Corrupts them how? How?

Mrs Grose I don't know, miss, I'm sure I don't, but I'm going to make that mug of Bengers. (*Going to the door of the dining-room*)

Miss Grey I tell you I don't want a mug of Bengers!

Mrs Grose No, but I do, miss. (*She opens the door, sees the dark and returns to the desk for her candle*) Beg pardon, miss.

Mrs Grose exits

Miss Grey stands in troubled thought for a long moment, then turns slowly to face the stairs

Miss Jessel stands on one of the lower steps. They exchange a long steady stare before Miss Jessel moves slowly upwards into the shadows and is gone

Miss Grey (*suddenly realizing the danger*) No! Flora! You won't have Flora! (*She takes a candle and climbs the stairs, moves along the landing and pauses listening at Flora's door. Then she opens the door quietly and stands on the threshold staring in*)

Downstairs Mrs Grose enters with a tray bearing mugs and candle

Mrs Grose There, the kettle won't be five minutes. (*She stops and looks about and grows scared*) Are you there, miss? Miss?

Behind her the curtains billow and she turns to stare at them, then backs slowly to the foot of the stairs. Miss Grey comes silently down and stands behind her

Miss Grey Mrs Grose.

Mrs Grose runs a few steps into the room before turning and staring

It's started again.

Mrs Grose No, please.

Miss Grey Yes. Here. On this very step. Not two minutes ago.

Mrs Grose Quint?

Miss Grey No, his woman. Standing here and trying to stare me out.
Mrs Grose What did you do, miss?
Miss Grey Why, I stared back. I stared the creature down. Do you think she frightens me? (*She comes down and points at the window*) What's more, there's another one of them out there.
Mrs Grose Another? No.
Miss Grey I tell you there's someone in the grounds, on the prowl.
Mrs Grose You mean you've seen——?
Miss Grey I ran up to see if Flora was safe – if that woman wasn't with her. And the child wasn't in her bed.
Mrs Grose Gone! Miss Flora! But merciful heavens!
Miss Grey Quiet, calm yourself. She hasn't gone anywhere. She's there, but she's standing at her window. She's just standing there looking out.
Mrs Grose At what?
Miss Grey At someone below in the garden. So wrapped up in the sight of it that she didn't even hear me open the door. She's standing there still.
Mrs Grose You didn't put the little mite back in her bed?
Miss Grey Hush! Of course not. We must see who it is she's communing with. If Flora can see it from her window, we can see it from this one. Open the curtains.
Mrs Grose What? I'd rather you did, miss.
Miss Grey I want you to see this time.
Mrs Grose Miss, my heart isn't as strong as yours.

Miss Grey goes to the window and carefully parts the curtains. She gazes out, then turns

Miss Grey It's horrible. It's worse than I dreamed.
Mrs Grose Who – what——?
Miss Grey Come. See.
Mrs Grose No, miss!
Miss Grey He's just standing there in the moonlight. Quite still.
Mrs Grose Draw the curtains, miss. We don't want him coming in here.
Miss Grey He wouldn't be interested in us. He's far too busy looking elsewhere. He's looking in the air.
Mrs Grose What – looking up at Miss Flora?
Miss Grey Higher. He's looking at somebody on the tower.
Mrs Grose What? Quint – looking up at Miss Jessel?
Miss Grey No, it isn't Quint. It's Miles.
Mrs Grose Miles? Out there?
Miss Grey Standing in the moonlight. Looking up with a smile on his face.
Mrs Grose But what can we do?
Miss Grey We can bring him in and find the truth at last.

She opens the window and goes out

Mrs Grose waits with a hand to her mouth

Soon Miles in slippers and dressing-gown comes calmly in, followed by Miss Grey, who closes the windows and draws the curtains

Miles (*with a smile*) Good-evening, Mrs Grose. Or is it good-morning?
Mrs Grose Whatever possessed you? Do you want to take your death of cold? (*She puts her shawl about his shoulders*)
Miles It isn't as cold as all that, to be honest.
Miss Grey Miles, what were you doing?

Miles gives her a big smile

No, Miles, a smile isn't good enough this time. What were you doing out there?
Miles I was being bad.

Pause

Miss Grey } (*together*) { What do you mean?
Mrs Grose } { But Miles——
Miss Grey Just a moment, Mrs Grose. What do you mean, Miles?
Miles It's simple. I was just being bad.
Miss Grey It isn't simple to me, Miles.
Miles I wanted to show you I could behave badly for once. You're both forever saying what an angel I am and it gets a chap down. It's as simple as that. (*He kisses them both*)
Miss Grey How long did you spend out there?
Miles I came down at midnight. When I'm bad I'm really bad.
Miss Grey And you thought all the time we'd find out?
Miles I knew you would. I fixed it with Flora.
Miss Grey How?
Miles She agreed to make a bump outside Mrs Grose's door.
Mrs Grose That was nice of you. Thank you very much, I'm obliged.
Miles I'm sorry, dear. It was only a lark. But it did show I could be bad, didn't it, if I tried?
Miss Grey It was very cleverly worked, Miles.
Mrs Grose It was downright foolish.
Miles Was it downright bad?
Mrs Grose It was downright disgraceful, that's what it was.
Miles But think for a moment—what I could do if I chose.

Pause

Mrs Grose Why, get off with you, you provoking puppet. Up those wooden hills to Bethlehem.
Miles Am I forgiven?
Miss Grey Yes. Go to bed now.
Mrs Grose I'll bring you a hot-water bottle—not that you deserve one, you mischievous elf.

Miles kisses them, then goes off upstairs to bed

There. And it was all a false alarm. There's always explanations for everything.

Miss Grey A false alarm? Is that all you think it was? Mrs Grose, you're the most magnificent monument to a want of imagination.

Mrs Grose What?

Miss Grey You didn't pick up his threat?

Mrs Grose Threat?

Miss Grey No, it passed you by. Those last few words he spoke. "Think for a moment," he said. "What I could do if I chose." It was a warning. It meant leave me alone or face the consequences. Those children haven't been good, Mrs Grose. They've only been absent. They're not ours. They're his and they're hers. But not for much longer. I'd see this house in ashes before I'd let those devils take those children. I'll save them, Mrs Grose.

Mrs Grose Save them from what, miss?

Miss Grey Why, isn't it obvious? From destruction. From damnation.

The Lights fade to a Black-out

ACT II

SCENE 1

The same. It is an autumn afternoon and the grey sky is darkening

Miles and Flora sit on the carpet beside a terrestrial globe. Miss Grey is knitting

Flora (*spinning the globe*) Just imagine, the earth is twenty-four thousand, nine hundred and one miles in circumference at the equator.

Miles And the surface area is one hundred and ninety-six million, five hundred and fifty-five thousand square miles.

Flora And there are fifty-five million, five hundred thousand square miles of land.

Miles And one-fifth of it belongs to the British Empire.

Flora Hooray!

Miles Britannia rules the waves!

Miss Grey Tell me somthing — were you both such tremendous prodigies of learning for Miss Jessel? (*She pauses*) Do you remember Miss Jessel?

Miles I suppose one-fifth of the world isn't all that much, really.

Flora No, why don't we have more? Why don't we own the River Amazon, Miss Grey? The longest river in the world?

Miles Four thousand miles. And the longest wall's in China — more than a thousand miles. Built in the year two hundred and fourteen before Christ.

Flora By the coolies. "Where tea is grown and rice is planted and coolies go with eyes so slanted." Miles could go out and bag it for England when he's grown up.

Miss Grey Children, I asked you a question.

Pause

Flora Miss Grey, tell us about Mrs Lavender and the wedding.

Miss Grey Oh no, not again, Flora.

Flora Oh please, just once more.

Miss Grey All right. It was when I was a little girl and we had a dreadfully slatternly woman who came in to clean every day——

Miles }
Flora } (*together*) Mrs Lavender!

Miss Grey Yes, Mrs Lavender. Well, one day, my papa took me to a wedding in the village and afterwards the most amazingly smart and grand lady came up to us, in splendid furs and feathers, and looking at me through——

Miles ⎫
Flora ⎭ (*together*)   A gold-rimmed *lorgnette*!

Miss Grey Yes, a gold-rimmed *lorgnette*. And Papa told me to shake hands with her but I was shy and I tried to hide behind his legs. And Papa said, "Come now, Evelyn, surely you know this lady?" And I said, "Yes, it's Queen Victoria." And Papa said, "Evelyn——"

Miles ⎫
Flora ⎭ (*together*)   It's Mrs Lavender! (*They roll with laughter*)

Miss Grey But you didn't answer my question about Miss Jessel.

Miles Tell us about the vicarage pony.

Flora Yes, tell us about Bertie.

Miss Grey Oh, no, not again. And it's nearly time for church.

Flora Tell us about Bertie and the roses.

Miss Grey Oh, all right. When Bertie first came to us and they put him in the field and he stood and watched me shut the latch on the paddock gate – watched terribly closely with his head on one side like this. And then, when we were all having lunch, Papa suddenly jumped up.

Flora And knocked his cup over!

Miss Grey Yes, because Bertie was in the garden eating all his prize tea roses.

Flora Yes, and your Papa made him eat nothing but tea roses for a whole week.

Miles Your father's a bit eccentric, isn't he, dear?

Miss Grey Eccentric? Yes, he is a little. Oh, well, poor Bertie's been dead and gone these many years, God bless him. Children, I wonder what happens to the creatures we love when they die? Do you think it's possible we might meet them again some day? (*She pauses*) I mean people who die, too.

Miles idly spins the globe

Miles?

Miles The largest inland sea is the Caspian.

Flora Yes, in Russia. (*She finds it on the globe*) There.

Miles One hundred and seventy thousand . . .

Miss Grey jumps up from her chair and goes to the window and stares out

Is anything the matter?

A pause. The children raise their brows

Mrs Grose comes in from the little hall wearing her Sunday finery

Mrs Grose We ought to be getting ready for church, miss. (*She pauses*) Miss? You know what the vicar's like if people walk in late.

Miss Grey (*turning angrily*) Yes, Mrs Grose – yes-yes-yes!

She walks out past the astonished Mrs Grose to the little hall

Mrs Grose Well, dear-dear-dear, what's wrong now?

Flora She's in one of her moods.

Miles Has she had a letter?

Mrs Grose goes to the window and glances out

Flora I wish I could hear from my family.

Miles Yes, why doesn't Uncle ever write? Why doesn't he come and see us?

Mrs Grose Uncle's a very, very busy man. Very. Now run along and put your coats on or you'll have the vicar standing in the pulpit and passing un-Christian remarks.

Miles (*stopping at the door*) Doesn't Uncle like us?

Miles Not like you? You silly darling, how could anybody resist you? (*She hugs and kisses them*) The dears, the darlings, the faithful creatures.

Miss Grey enters in hat and coat and carrying gloves and Bible

Now shoo the pair of you, and get ready. (*She shoos them out*)

Miles and Flora exit to the little hall

(*Closing the door*) I wish their uncle would spare them the occasional day. They're the saddest little orphans in Christendom.

Miss Grey Are they?

Mrs Grose What do you mean by that?

Miss Grey I thought you were aware of my feelings.

Mrs Grose What—but surely you don't still believe—? Upon my soul, miss, there's been nothing amiss for ages and ages—not since Master Miles got up to his little prank in the garden.

Miss Grey Hasn't there?

Mrs Grose You mean there has?

Miss Grey Two nights ago, when I was sitting up reading, I happened to look up from my book and she was there—there on the stairs.

Mrs Grose Miss Jessel? What—what time of night might this have been?

Miss Grey Was I asleep, you mean? Was it a nightmare? Is that all it ever is?

Mrs Grose No, miss, I swear——

Miss Grey But you had the thought and who can blame you? Nobody else has seen them. Why does it always have to be me—only me? Why on earth do you never see anything? Or perhaps you do.

Mrs Grose No, miss.

Miss Grey But she was there—there—as solid as those banisters. I could draw you a picture. The way she sat—her beautiful dark hair—her poor thin wrists.

Mrs Grose Sat? She was sitting down?

Miss Grey She was sitting on the stairs and she was crying. (*She goes and sits on one of the lower stairs*) Here. Her face was in her arm and she was sobbing. Like this. And her other hand was holding the rail, like this, because I remember thinking what a slender wrist she had, like a boy's. Did Miss Jessel have slender wrists, normal wrists?

Mrs Grose Thin, miss, like a child's.

Miss Grey So do you still think I was dreaming?

Mrs Grose But the children—they haven't been naughty?

Miss Grey No.

Mrs Grose Well—there.

Miss Grey But would we see if they were? They're so evasive. Every time I mention Quint or Miss Jessel or Miles's school they simply change the subject. Only just now, I tested them. I asked about Miss Jessel. I asked if we'd ever see our loved ones again once they were dead.

Mrs Grose Heavens! You asked those poor orphans about the dead?

Miss Grey And do you think they answered me? No, they just wriggled out of it.

Mrs Grose Miss! Wouldn't anybody wriggle out of such a dreadful subject?

Miss Grey I swear to you, Mrs Grose, there are times when I'm certain that in my presence, but without me being able to see, those children have visitors. Visitors who are known and welcome. Because whatever I see, they see more. Sometimes I want to cry out to them, "They're here, they're here, you little wretches, and you can't deny it now!" I want to—— (*She breaks off as the door opens*)

Miles and Flora enter dressed for church

Flora Has anybody seen my mittens, please?

Mrs Grose They're in the hall table, darling. I picked them up in the garden.

Flora Oh, yes.

She goes out to the little hall

Mrs Grose Put something warmer on, Miles. It's autumn now and it's a topcoat colder.

Miles My tweed coat? It's in my wardrobe.

Mrs Grose Well run up and get it out of your wardrobe, child.

Miles goes quickly up to his room

That vicar puts the fear of God into me.

Miss Grey Well, you walk ahead with Flora and we'll catch you up.

Mrs Grose You wouldn't mind?

Miss Grey No, I don't have such an elevated idea of clergymen as you.

Mrs Grose Don't you, miss? No. All right. Don't be too long.

She hurries out to the little hall

Miles comes down buttoning his tweed coat. He has a matching cap in his pocket

Miss Grey Let me button you up. (*She fastens his top button*) There.

He steps back and they stare at one another

Are you ready?

Miles Do you mind if I ask you something?

Miss Grey No.

Miles (*smiling*) When in the world am I going back to school? You know, my dear, for a chap to be with a lady all the time ...

Miss Grey And always the same lady?

Miles Well of course she's a very nice lady, but after all I'm getting on now. And you can't say I haven't been frightfully good, can you?

Miss Grey Can't I?

Miles Well, except for that one night.

Miss Grey Which night?

Miles You know—when I came down—when I stood in the garden.

Miss Grey Oh, yes. I forget why you did that.

Miles You forget? It was to show you I could.

Miss Grey Oh, yes, Miles, you could.

Miles And I could again.

Miss Grey Yes, but you won't.

Miles No, not that again. That was nothing.

Miss Grey Come on, Miles, we'll be late.

Miles When *am* I going back?

Miss Grey Were you happy at school?

Miles I'm happy anywhere as long as I'm left alone.

Miss Grey Well, if you're just as happy here as elsewhere.

Miles But that isn't everything. Of course, you know a lot.

Miss Grey But you know almost as much?

Miles I don't know half as much as I want to. But it isn't just that. I want to see more life. I want my own sort.

Miss Grey There aren't many of your sort, Miles. Except perhaps Flora.

Miles What? A baby girl?

Miss Grey But don't you love little Flora?

Miles Of course I do. If I didn't—and you as well—if I didn't——

Miss Grey Yes? If you didn't?

Miles Well, you know what!

Miss Grey I only wish I did. What do you mean, Miles?

Miles (*smiling*) Oh, nothing. Does Uncle think what you think?

Miss Grey How do you know what I think?

Miles Well I don't, obviously, because you never tell me, do you? But I mean—does Uncle know?

Miss Grey Know what?

Miles The way I'm going on.

Miss Grey And how are you going on?

Miles You keep saying that, but you know, you know.

Miss Grey Yes, I know, Miles, but I'd like to hear it from your own lips. And then we can start putting it right. Don't you understand? I can do nothing to save you if you won't be frank with me. Don't you want to be saved?

Miles Saved? What do you mean? Saved from what?

Miss Grey (*taking hold of him*) Miles, I only want to help you. I'd rather die than do you a wrong or cause you pain. But you must help me to save you.

Miles (*getting away*) No, let me go! I want to get away from here.

Miss Grey No, Miles.

Miles Yes. If you don't let me go my uncle will have to come down and settle it once and for all.

Miss Grey (*taken aback*) Your uncle?

Miles Yes, you wouldn't like that, would you? You'd have to tell him an awful lot, wouldn't you? He wouldn't be very pleased with you, would he?
Miss Grey Do you think you can threaten me with your uncle?
Miles I'm not threatening. I'm just saying we'll have him down here to sort everything out. If you lose his golden opinion that's just jolly hard luck on you.
Miss Grey I see, Miles. Either I inform your uncle or I leave you alone to carry on exactly as you wish.
Miles We'll just have him down here and see, shall we?
Miss Grey And who'll get him to come down?
Miles (*bright and emphatic*) I will.

He puts on his cap then strolls out to the little hall, leaving the door open

Miss Grey stares after him, then calls

Miss Grey No, Miles! Don't think you can frighten me with your uncle. I know your little schemes.

The front door is heard slamming

Very well. Go to church yourself. (*She takes off her hat*) And don't forget to say your prayers, because you need them. (*She closes the door, then looks up and around and addresses invisible spirits afloat in the air*) All right, you devils. Did you hear all that? Did it amuse you? Are you pleased with your pupil? Did he acquit himself perfectly in accordance with your instructions? Were you pleased with his evasions and his lies and his threats? (*She moves to the stairs. Calling up*) For God's sake, why don't you leave them in peace? (*She pauses*) Why don't you answer? Why don't you come now and face me? There's no-one else here. Only me. Or must I come up there and find you? (*She pauses*) I'm waiting. (*She pauses*) Very well, I'll come to you. (*She goes to the desk and finds the key, lights a candle and starts to mount the stairs. She stops halfway, her resolution gone, and turns in tears*) I can't. I can't do it. (*She grips a banister rail and subsides on the step in the manner of the woe-stricken Miss Jessel, her head sunk in the crook of her elbow. After a moment she turns to see her hand holding the rail and slowly opens the fingers wide, then snatches the hand away*) Oh, God, let me not be mad. (*She goes slowly to the centre of the room, then turns and shouts*) All right! You've beaten me! I'm leaving! I can't stand one more hour of this place! (*She runs upstairs and for a time the room is deserted. Five o'clock strikes. She hurries down with a hastily packed bag trailing items of clothing. She snatches up and packs letters and other small possessions, puts on her hat, fastens her bag and goes to the door. Then she remembers something else*) My music case. (*She crosses to the schoolroom door and opens it — then steps back in horror*) So. You were there all the time. (*She backs into the room*)

Miss Jessel appears on the threshold

They stare

Listen to me, you poor miserable woman. Why can't you leave them alone? Because I'll never let you have them, you know.

Miss Jessel comes a step closer

You won't drive me away. I'll stay. I'll stay for ever if need be.

Miss Jessel holds out her arms beseechingly and takes another step towards Miss Grey as the Lights fade to a Black-out

SCENE 2

The same. It is two hours later and the room is lit by the moon

Miss Grey sits staring ahead in her hat and coat. Her bag is on the floor. The front door is heard opening

Mrs Grose (*off*) Come on, my dears, in you go. It bites your face off out there.

The front door is heard closing

Flora (*off*) Where's Miss Grey? Do you think she's ill?
Mrs Grose (*off*) Take your coats off and we'll soon find out.

    The door from the little hall is opened and Mrs Grose stands on the threshold

    Miss Grey? Is anybody there? (*Advancing a step*) Hello, are you there, dear?

    Miles and Flora enter

Miss Grey Yes, I'm here, Mrs Grose.
Miles (*whispering*) Why is she sitting in the dark?
Mrs Grose Shh! Now get out of here and take off your coats. Go on. Miss Grey doesn't want to be disturbed.
Flora Why not? What's the matter?
Mrs Grose Now do as you're told, Miss Flora. Out

    Mrs Grose follows Flora and Miles out. In a short while she returns holding a lighted candle. She goes to Miss Grey and holds the light to her face

    Miss, whatever's the matter? You didn't come to church.
Miss Grey No, I stayed here to meet a friend.
Mrs Grose A friend?
Miss Grey Oh, yes, I have a couple, you know.
Mrs Grose Do you, miss?
Miss Grey Oh, yes. (*Rising*) Where are Flora and Miles?
Mrs Grose (*lighting the lamp*) Gone to the kitchen for their suppers. (*When the lamp is lit she goes to the window and closes the curtains. On the way back she stumbles over Miss Grey's bag and picks it up*) What's the meaning of this, miss?
Miss Grey As you see, I packed my bag.

Mrs Grose (*dismayed*) Packed your bag? To go, you mean? To leave us? No, you mustn't, miss! You can't just abandon us like that!

Miss Grey No, of course I can't.

Mrs Grose You mean you'll stay?

Miss Grey Of course I'll stay! I had a moment of panic, that's all, which is exactly what they were counting on. Oh, they're so very subtle, Mrs Grose. They keep turning the screw another little notch until I'm screaming inside my head. But I've no intention of quitting. I propose to fight on. And it's not just the children I'm thinking of. It's my own peace of mind. Imagine what it would do to me if I ran away with all these questions left dangling. I'd spend the rest of my life wondering if it all really happened or if once upon a time I went mad for a season — like a hare. I'd keep asking myself if I suffered from some sickness that might break out again without warning and ruin my happiness — if I ever found happiness. How could I risk having children of my own if I suspected there was some twisted corner in my mind that conjured up horrible visions where there was nothing but innocence and goodness? How could I stand the torment of thinking it was some terrible derangement that could be handed down from one generation to the next like a bad chest? Why talk of bad chests? We both know I mean insanity. I am not mad, said the lemming, I just love death leaps. (*She pauses, then she laughs*) Oh, don't look so solemn, Mrs Grose. I think I'm healthy enough. Although you might think otherwise when you hear what I've got to say next.

Mrs Grose And what's that, miss?

Miss Grey I told you I stayed here to meet a friend?

Mrs Grose Yes, miss?

Miss Grey It was Miss Jessel. (*She pauses*) Yes, I stayed here for a talk with Miss Jessel.

Mrs Grose What? And she came?

Miss Grey Oh, yes, she came.

Mrs Grose And she spoke to you?

Miss Grey As well as a dead woman can speak.

Mrs Grose Merciful powers. And what did she say to you?

Miss Grey She said she suffers the torments of the damned and she comes here because she wants to share them.

Mrs Grose To share them?

Miss Grey To share them with Flora.

Mrs Grose No, miss! It's me that's going to lose my mind!

Miss Grey takes her by the shoulders

Miss Grey No, Mrs Grose, you mustn't fail me now. You're the sweetest and most faithful human soul and you've kept me from losing my balance all this time, so promise you won't break when I need you most, when we all need you.

Mrs Grose But if that terrible woman wants Flora!

Miss Grey Mrs Grose, it doesn't matter.

Mrs Grose It doesn't matter?

Miss Grey It doesn't matter because I've made up my mind.

Mrs Grose Made it up to do what?

Miss Grey To send for their uncle.

Mrs Grose Oh, miss, do, for pity's sake.

Miss Grey I'm going to. There's nothing else for it. Miles thinks I daren't but this time he's made a miscalculation. Mr Crimond will come down and hear it all from me on the spot — and in front of Miles himself. In the first place I'll show him the letter from the school.

Mrs Grose (*dismayed*) What? Show it to the master?

Miss Grey As I should have done in the first place.

Mrs Grose No, miss!

Miss Grey Yes. And I'll put it to him squarely that he can't hope to live in happy ignorance when his ward has been dismissed from school.

Mrs Grose Dismissed for being too good and clever, that's all, miss!

Miss Grey No, Mrs Grose, for wickedness.

Mrs Grose No, I'll never hear that said, miss!

Miss Grey For what else then? When he's so accomplished and beautiful and charming? At any rate I'll bring the whole thing out in the open. After all, it was their uncle's fault. If he deliberately turns his back and leaves such monsters here to corrupt those he's charged with protecting——

Mrs Grose But he had no idea! He didn't know they were monsters! No, and that's my fault!

Miss Grey Well I'll see you don't suffer.

Mrs Grose The children then — are they to suffer?

Miss Grey I'll tell the plain truth.

Mrs Grose Couldn't you soften it a little for their sakes? Those babies mean no harm, miss.

Miss Grey So I tell him a story that's been carefully abridged and altered and full of soothing syrup to cover their blemishes? One might as well say nothing at all and leave him in peace while they go to the devil.

Mrs Grose But you needn't tell him at all. I'll tell him.

Miss Grey You'll write? I thought you couldn't.

Mrs Grose No, miss, I can't. I tell the bailiff. He writes for me.

Miss Grey You'd like to tell the bailiff our story?

Pause

Mrs Grose (*defeated*) No, miss. You write.

Miss Grey I'm going to, right away. (*She sits at the desk*) Good-night, Mrs Grose. See that I'm not disturbed.

Mrs Grose Miss — the children — don't be too hard on them. They're only babies.

Miss Grey I know what they are, Mrs Grose. Good-night.

Mrs Grose bobs a curtsy and goes out

Miss Grey picks up a pen and thinks, as the Lights fade to a Black-out

SCENE 3

The same. It is late afternoon on the following day. The Lights fade during the scene, as evening falls

Miles is heard playing the piano off in the schoolroom. Flora is painting at an easel by the window. Mrs Grose is her model, draped in a white sheet and holding an orange in her outstretched hand, one foot raised from the ground behind her, one hand resting on a chair for support

Mrs Grose Merciful powers, Miss Flora, how much longer am I supposed to stand like this? It's nothing short of torture.

Flora (*amused*) Do be patient! I'm just trying to paint the folds in your flowing robes and it's awfully tricky. Every time you move I have to start again.

Mrs Grose Well can't I stand on the other leg for five minutes? I'm getting the cramps in this one something shocking.

Flora No, just stand exactly as you are and stop complaining. And hold that orange steady. It keeps going up and down like the sun rising and setting.

Mrs Grose What am I supposed to be, anyway?

Flora Patience on a Monument.

Mrs Grose Well I can't stand here all day. I wish Miss Grey would hurry up and then she could take my place.

Flora Look, you can go if you like and I'll paint it from imagination.

Mrs Grose You know quite well I've got strict orders to stay here and keep an eye on you till she comes back from her walk.

Flora I won't go anywhere. I'll just stay here painting. Go on. You must have lots to do.

Mrs Grose No, miss, I've got my instructions. Oh, this poor leg. It's full of pins and needles now.

Flora Keep your hand steady. The sun's sinking again.

Mrs Grose So am I sinking. Is she still walking up and down that garden?

Flora (*glancing out*) Walking and walking – up and down – up and down. Why doesn't she go for a proper walk in the country?

Mrs Grose Doesn't want to stir too far away from you.

Flora Why not?

Mrs Grose Because she's so fond of you.

Flora Well why didn't she take us out with her?

Mrs Grose She's got a lot of thinking to do.

Flora What about?

Mrs Grose Leos for meddlers and crutches for lame ducks.

Flora Why did she miss church last night?

Mrs Grose Nasty headache. Now get on with your picture before my leg falls asleep.

Flora Miles thought it was his fault. He thought he said something by accident that upset her. Something she took the wrong way. He was dreadfully upset because he adores her. Miss Grey's a little strange, isn't she?

Mrs Grose Strange?

The piano music stops during the next few speeches

Flora Eccentric. But of course all her family are as well.

Mrs Grose (*abandoning her pose*) Eccentric?

Flora Yes, they sound very peculiar, all of them.

Mrs Grose What do you mean, child?

Flora Her papa sounds quite unhinged.

Mrs Grose Unhinged? Get away with you. He's a clerk in holy orders.

Flora What difference does that make? And I don't think her sisters are much better. Miss Grey herself behaves very oddly sometimes. Have you noticed? How she jumps on one for no reason at all and asks strange questions?

Mrs Grose Don't you like Miss Grey?

Flora Oh, yes, I love her, but sometimes she frightens me. Perhaps it just comes from all those strange books she reads.

Mrs Grose What books?

Flora Oh, spooky ones. She gobbles them like strawberries. Novels about ghosts and madwomen locked up in attic rooms. She sits up half the night and reads nothing else. *The Mysteries of Udolpho* and *Jane Eyre* and things like that. Shall I tell you what I think?

Mrs Grose Well?

Flora I think she's got a very vivid imagination. Have you ever noticed her eyes?

Mrs Grose What about her eyes?

Flora It's as though she can see something that we can't.

Miss Grey enters through the window wearing her hat and coat

Miss Grey Hello. It's getting jolly cold. (*She pauses*) Is anything the matter, Mrs Grose?

Mrs Grose No, miss.

Miss Grey (*removing her hat and coat*) You were giving me such a strange look. Miles? Mrs Grose, where's Miles?

Mrs Grose He's in the schoolroom playing the piano.

Miss Grey Piano? Can you hear any piano?

Mrs Grose (*listening*) He must have stopped.

Miss Grey Oh, you foolish woman. I knew I should never have trusted you. (*She opens the schoolroom door*) Miles, will you come in here now?

Miles plays a final flourish on the piano

Forgive me for being sharp, Mrs Grose, but there is a method in my—— (*She stops herself*)

Mrs Grose A reason for your precautions? Yes, miss, I understand, miss. Let me take your things. (*She takes Miss Grey's hat and coat and heads for the door to the little hall, still sheeted*)

Miles enters from the schoolroom and raises his arm to her in Roman salute

Miles Hail, mighty Caesar! Beware the ides of March.

Mrs Grose And you keep a civil tongue in your head, Master Miles.

Miles I shall remember, O Emperor. When Caesar says "Do this" it is performed.

Mrs Grose All right, catch this. (*She tosses him the orange and goes out*)

Miles I ought to have called her the wife to Caesar but I couldn't think of the name. (*He thinks*) Calpurnia!

Miss Grey Calpurnia?

Miles Yes, Caesar's wife — Calpurnia.

Miss Grey Where do you pick up all your curious knowledge, Miles?

Miles Oh, here and there. I read. Why?

Miss Grey Sometimes one might almost think you were being secretly instructed by somebody else.

Miles Anybody knows who Caesar's wife was.

Miss Grey Do they?

Miles Even little old Flo.

Miss Grey It wouldn't surprise me at all.

Miles Are you still cross with me?

Miss Grey I've never been cross with you, Miles.

Miles No, but I upset you. I'm sorry. (*He kisses her*) I only said I wanted to go back to school and have Uncle down for a visit.

Miss Grey He'll be down shortly, so you'll have your wish.

Miles Uncle? Coming here?

Miss Grey Well, I've written to him.

Miles Oh, what did you say?

Miss Grey Quite enough, Miles.

A pause

Miles Marvellous. So we're friends again?

Miss Grey Why, were we foes?

Miles Never. The best of friends, always. (*He kisses her*) I composed you a little song this afternoon as a peace offering.

Miss Grey Really?

Miles I don't suppose you want to hear it?

Miss Grey For me? Truly?

Miles Well, it's called *Miss Grey's Polonaise*. It's a dance, actually, in three-four time.

Miss Grey How flattering. I'm honoured.

Miles It's rubbish, actually.

Miss Grey I'm sure it isn't, Miles.

Miles Wait till you hear it and then say it isn't. Come on.

Miles leads Miss Grey into the schoolroom and soon the piano is heard, off

Flora goes to the desk, takes out the key of the tower, closes the drawer, tiptoes up the stairs and exits

It grows darker

Miss Grey puts her head out of the schoolroom

Miss Grey Flora, come and hear Miles's song.

The piano stops

Flora? (*Coming into the room*) Flora? (*Going back to the schoolroom door*) Miles, where's Flora?

Miles (*off*) How should I know? (*He laughs and his laughter grows into a wild incoherent song, accompanied by the piano. This frenzied dance accompanies Miss Grey's search*)

Miss Grey opens the window and stands on the terrace looking for Flora

Miss Grey Flora! Flora! (*She comes in and bangs the windows shut, then runs up to Flora's room and opens the door*) Flora! Flora! (*She hurries down, opens the little hall door and calls*) Mrs Grose! Mrs Grose, come here! (*She remembers the dining-room door and rushes to it*) Flora? Are you in there? (*Turning*) They tricked me, the little devils tricked me. Miles! Stop that blessed noise!

The piano stops

Mrs Grose comes in, with a lighted candle

Mrs Grose Merciful heavens, miss, what is it?

Miss Grey Oh, what an idiot! I think I am mad.

Mrs Grose Why, miss?

Miss Grey It's Flora. I turned my back for no more than a minute and she gave me the slip.

Mrs Grose She'll be up above, in her room.

Miss Grey Don't you think I've looked in her room? But you're right, yes, she is above.

Mrs Grose In the tower?

Miss Grey I know she is, and she's with that woman.

Mrs Grose What, and Miles, too?

Miss Grey Miles? Of course not. He's with Quint.

Mrs Grose Quint?

Miss Grey They're in there.

Mrs Grose But miss, are you going to let him——?

Miss Grey Stay alone in there with Quint? Yes, it doesn't matter now. Get me the key to the tower, quickly.

Mrs Grose searches in the drawer and finally shakes her head

No, because Flora took it. The trick's been played. He found the most divine little excuse to keep me quiet while she slipped away.

Mrs Grose Divine, miss?

Miss Grey Infernal, then. And at the same time he provided for himself. Now bring that candle and follow me.

Mrs Grose Do you really think that little girl's ventured up into that terrible dark place all alone?

Miss Grey She's not alone; and at times like this she's not a child. She's an old, old woman. (*She goes to the stairs*)

Mrs Grose (*hanging back*) And you think Miss Jessel's up there, too?

Miss Grey Think? I'm certain. And you're about to see with your own eyes, Mrs Grose.

Mrs Grose Thank you, miss, I'm sure.

Miss Grey Well, are you coming?

Mrs Grose gives her the candle and follows her up the stairs

Stop. (*She raises the candle*)

Flora comes down into the light

Mrs Grose brushes past Miss Grey and hugs the child

Mrs Grose There she is all the time, the dear, the darling, the little faithful.

Miss Grey descends and watches the couple on the stairs. Flora stares back blankly, then descends hand in hand with Mrs Grose. They stare at Miss Grey

Miss Grey Well, Flora?

Pause

Did you have a good time up there?

Pause

And did Miss Jessel enjoy your company?

Mrs Grose No, miss, you mustn't! You've made a mistake!

Miss Grey And where is she now, Flora? Where is your friend Miss Jessel?

Mrs Grose Miss—please!

Miss Grey You don't wish to tell me, Flora? No matter. Because she's there—she's there. (*She points up the stairs*)

Miss Jessel appears at the top of the stairs

Mrs Grose turns to look. Flora gazes at Miss Grey

She's there, you unhappy little thing. There, there, there. And you see her as well as you see me.

Mrs Grose But, miss, there's nothing! Nothing!

Miss Grey Nothing?

Mrs Grose Nothing, miss. Now don't go frightening the child.

Miss Grey What? You don't see her, exactly as we do? You mean to say you don't now—now? But she's as big as a blazing fire. Look again. You must look again.

Mrs Grose looks, then puts her arms round Flora

Mrs Grose There, there, don't worry your head, my cherub. She isn't there and nobody's there and you don't see nothing, my sweet. It's all just a silly mistake and a worry and a joke.

Flora (*to Miss Grey*) I don't know what you mean. I see nobody. I see nothing. I never have. I think you're cruel. I don't like you. Take me away! Oh, take me away from her!

Miss Grey From me?

Flora From you! Yes! From you!

Miss Grey Flora, my dear, let me tell you something before you go. If ever I had fears for my sanity you've just dispelled them all.

Flora I want to go!

Miss Grey I know you do. You're so much in her power that I've lost you. Goodbye, Flora.

Flora sobs in Mrs Grose's arms

Well go, then. Go! (*She hands the candle to Mrs Grose*)

Mrs Grose leads Flora up to her room. They walk straight past Miss Jessel, who looks down at Miss Grey before disappearing as the candlelight moves away

Miss Grey lights the lamp and sits on the chaise-longue *staring grimly ahead. She takes no notice when the schoolroom door opens*

Miles stands on the threshold with a troubled face

Miles (*nervously*) Miss Grey?

She pays him no attention. He comes in nervously and finally sits at the other end of the chaise-longue. *He turns to her with a small gesture of appeal but she looks away and they sit there in silence for a while*

Mrs Grose comes down and pauses to take in the strained scene

Mrs Grose Miles?

Pause

Master Miles?

At last he turns

You'd better have an early night, too. Come on. I'll put your supper on a tray.

Miles turns in appeal to Miss Grey. She refuses to look at him and he goes to the stairs

Miss Grey And Mrs Grose?

Mrs Grose Yes, miss?

Miss Grey See that he doesn't speak to Flora.

Mrs Grose I've locked her door, miss.

Miss Grey Good-night, Miles, and don't forget to say your prayers.

Miles walks past Mrs Grose, who lays a pitying hand on his passing shoulder

He goes upstairs and exits to his room

Does she still claim she saw nothing? That she's never seen anything?

Mrs Grose Miss, how could I ask her such things?

Miss Grey So you're on their side. And I'm mad.

Mrs Grose No, miss, I think not.

Miss Grey I'm not mad?

Mrs Grose No.

Miss Grey Why not?

Mrs Grose Because I believe she did see — what you said.

Miss Grey What makes you say that?

Mrs Grose The change that's come over her. The terrible change. In the last few minutes Miss Flora's turned quite old, every inch of her. Old and ugly and not my Miss Flora at all.

Miss Grey And I suppose she wants to get rid of me.

Mrs Grose She says she never wants to see your face again.

Miss Grey So you've come to speed me on my way? No, I've got a better idea. It's you that must go, Mrs Grose.

Mrs Grose Me?

Miss Grey Yes, and take her with you. Away from here. Away from them.

Mrs Grose But where can we go?

Miss Grey Straight to her uncle.

Mrs Grose But she'll just go and tell on you.

Miss Grey I know. She's got her grievance against me, which is exactly what she wanted, and she'll play it for all it's worth. She'll tell him I'm mad. But that doesn't matter now. You've got to leave me here to work out the remedy.

Mrs Grose Remedy? But what is the remedy?

Miss Grey The remedy depends on Miles and that's why I must be alone with him.

Mrs Grose But what if he should turn on you?

Miss Grey I'm not sure. I can't be sure of anything but you. But I've seen one ray of hope. Did you notice the poor wretch sitting here just now? He was reaching out to me. He wanted to tell me something, but you came down before he could bring himself to say it. So if you go and leave me alone with him . . .

Mrs Grose I'll go first thing in the morning.

Miss Grey If you want to stay, I'll go.

Mrs Grose I couldn't stay.

Miss Grey Couldn't?

Mrs Grose Not in this house.

Miss Grey Do you mean *you've* seen something?

Mrs Grose It's not what I've seen, it's what I've just heard.

Miss Grey And what's that?

Mrs Grose Language. From that child.

Miss Grey Flora?

Mrs Grose Wicked, horrible language. The most vile and dreadful talk I ever heard.

Miss Grey Was it about me?

Mrs Grose Yes, miss.

Miss Grey She slandered me?

Mrs Grose It was more than slander. It was evil. Such words. I can't think wherever she picked them up.

Miss Grey Can't you? Well I can.

Mrs Grose So can I, miss, but I can't bear it. I can't bear it from the sweet-faced little soul.

Miss Grey But if you can't bear it how can you stay with her?

Mrs Grose That's why I must, miss—to get her away—from this—from them.

Miss Grey So you do believe?

Mrs Grose In them? I have to. I've been forced to believe.

Miss Grey Thank God.

Mrs Grose Thank God?

Miss Grey That I'm not mad.

Mrs Grose It's not you that's mad. It's this place. Mad and bad and not to be borne by innocent children. I'd best go and take a look at her now.

Miss Grey Yes, don't leave her alone.

Mrs Grose I'll sleep in her room.

Miss Grey You're a good woman, Mrs Grose.

Mrs Grose You're a little Trojan yourself. We'll leave for her uncle's straight after breakfast.

Miss Grey My letter will be there before you.

Mrs Grose Letter?

Miss Grey About Miles.

Mrs Grose No, miss, it never went.

Miss Grey What do you mean? Why not?

Mrs Grose It went missing.

Miss Grey You mean someone took it? You mean Miles?

Mrs Grose I put it on the hall table this morning for the messenger to collect. But when he called again this afternoon and I asked if he'd picked it up he said he'd never seen it.

Miss Grey I see. So Miles has read it, and probably destroyed it.

Mrs Grose And you see what that means, miss? It tells us what he did at that school of his and why they sent him home. He stole.

Miss Grey Possibly.

Mrs Grose He did, miss. He just stole letters.

Miss Grey Well I hope it gave him more satisfaction than stealing mine did. It was nothing but a request for an interview.

Mrs Grose Maybe that's what he wanted to confess to you just now.

Miss Grey I wonder. But don't worry. I'll have it out of him once you and Flora are safely out of the way. He'll confess. And if only he confesses, he's saved. And if he's saved——

Mrs Grose Then so are you? Never you mind, miss, I'll save you without his help. (*She kisses Miss Grey*) Good-night, miss.
Miss Grey Good-night.
Mrs Grose You're sure you can face it all by yourself? It could be a stormy passage.
Miss Grey Yes, "So foul a sky clears not without a storm." I'll have to face it. But so will they.

Mrs Grose starts up the stairs, as the Lights fade to a Black-out

SCENE 4

The same. It is dusk the following day

Miss Grey stands at the window looking out. She sees something, opens the window and hurries into the dining-room

Miles comes in through the window with his hat on his head and his coat over his shoulder

Miss Grey returns with a supper tray. When she speaks she strives for a pleasant normality

Miss Grey Welcome home.

Pause

Where have you been all day?

Pause

Well, have you lost your tongue?
Miles I've been for a stroll.
Miss Grey A stroll, lasting from breakfast time to sunset?
Miles I just felt like a good long walk.
Miss Grey All by yourself?
Miles Yes.
Miss Grey I thought you might have been with a friend.
Miles I haven't got any friends. I only had Flora and now she's gone.
Miss Grey I thought you might have had some other friends.
Miles Did you? Well I haven't, actually.

Miss Grey closes the window, then takes his hat and coat and tidies them away on a chair

Miss Grey What did you do about food?
Miss Grey I took some apples.
Miss Grey And drink?
Miles I drank out of a stream.
Miss Grey (*indicating the tray*) Well now you can have some real food. You must be starving.

Miles takes a plate of food and sits down and eats hungrily. Miss Grey pours him a glass of milk

I was very worried when you didn't come in for your lessons.
Miles Sorry.
Miss Grey Of course it's silly to go on pretending that I've anything more to teach you. You've quite overtaken me in all sorts of ways. But you might have let me know you intended staying out all day. What was I to think?
Miles Yes, I'm sorry. I won't do it again.
Miss Grey Is your supper all right?
Miles It's jolly good. Thank you.
Miss Grey Miles, listen to me. I meant what I said about having nothing more to teach you. Except for one thing. And that's to *use* your intelligence. If you use it properly it can save you. It can help you to overcome any evil influences you might meet on your journey through life. It's your best weapon. Do you understand, Miles?
Miles Yes, and it can keep a chap from poverty and starvation. I say, Miss Grey.
Miss Grey Yes, Miles?
Miles Is little Flo *very* poorly?
Miss Grey No, she'll soon be back in fighting trim. London will do her good. Bly didn't agree with her.
Miles What, all of a sudden, just like that? Overnight?
Miss Grey No, not overnight. It had been coming on for some time.
Miles Why didn't you pack her off before, then?
Miss Grey Before what?
Miles Before she became too ill to travel?
Miss Grey But she wasn't. She only had a headache and a fever. The journey will most likely blow away the bad influences. And with God's help they won't trouble her again.
Miles I hope not. (*He puts down his plate and stands*) So — we're all alone!
Miss Grey Yes, we appear to be.
Miles It doesn't upset you, does it? Being alone with me?
Miss Grey Why should it upset me? You're the best company in the world. Why else do you think I stay?
Miles Is that all you stay for?
Miss Grey I stay because I'm your friend and because of the great interest I take in your well-being until something can be found that's more worthy of you. Don't you remember me telling you once before, the night I missed going to church, that there was nothing I wouldn't do for you? Nothing in the world?
Miles That was so I'd do something for *you.*
Miss Grey Partly. And you didn't do it, did you? Do you remember what it was?
Miles You wanted me to tell you something.
Miss Grey To tell me what you have on your mind, yes. And I'm still waiting for the answer.

Miles Is that why you've stayed?

Miss Grey Very well, if we're being honest with each other, yes. Would you like to talk about it?

Miles What, now?

Miss Grey When better? Let's clear the air.

Miles holds his head as though it aches

What's the matter?

Miles I think I've caught a spot of Flo's fever. (*He shakes his head as though to clear it*) Look, I'll tell you everything. And you'll stay here with me and we'll both be all right. Honestly, I will tell you, but not yet.

Miss Grey Why not, Miles?

Miles I need some fresh air.

Miss Grey All right, go for a little walk in the garden and collect your thoughts and I'll wait here for you. Then you can come back and tell me everything. Is that a bargain?

Miles Yes.

Miss Grey Before I let you go, will you do something for me in return? Something smaller?

Miles Much smaller?

Miss Grey The smallest fraction.

Miles All right.

Miss Grey Tell me if, yesterday afternoon, from the table in the hall, you took, you know, my letter.

Miles Your letter? Letter?

Quint appears at the window

Miss Grey springs forward to hold Miles by the shoulders and keep him with his back to the window

Miss Grey Miles, stay exactly as you are. Don't look behind you.

Miles tries to turn

No! Keep your eyes on mine. This is very important, Miles. Listen to me and take no notice of any other voices you might hear. Just tell me the truth and you'll be saved. Now tell me, Miles, and may God forgive you if you lie: did you take my letter?

Pause

Miles!

Miles Yes. Yes, I took it.

Quint makes a slow wheel like the prowl of a baffled beast

Miss Grey Fine, Miles! Splendid! You're winning! Now, keep telling the whole truth. What did you take it for?

Pause

Why did you take my letter?
Miles To see what it said about me.
Miss Grey You opened it?
Miles Yes, I opened it.

Quint vanishes

Miss Grey (*embracing Miles*) There! Thank God, thank God, we've won! You see, all it needs is the truth. And what did you do with the letter?
Miles I burnt it.
Miss Grey Splendid!
Miles Splendid?
Miss Grey That you've owned up. Now, Miles, tell me everything. Tell me the truth, the plain truth, and you're saved, I promise you, and there'll be no more worries and no more fears and you'll start with a clean slate and we'll all be happy together. Now tell me, honestly, is that what you did at school?
Miles At school?
Miss Grey Did you take letters? Or other things?
Miles Do you mean did I steal?
Miss Grey Yes. You must tell me. Is that why they expelled you?
Miles No, I never stole anything.
Miss Grey Then what did you do?

Pause

Well?
Miles I said things.
Miss Grey You said things? Is that all?
Miles Well, they thought it was enough.
Miss Grey Enough to expel you?
Miles Well I shouldn't have said them, should I?
Miss Grey Who did you say them to?
Miles I don't know. I can't remember.
Miss Grey Why? Did you say them to so many?
Miles No, just the boys I liked.
Miss Grey The boys you liked? What, and these boys you liked repeated them?
Miles They must have done. To the boys they liked.
Miss Grey Until in the end they came to the ears of the masters?
Miles Yes, but I didn't think they'd tell.
Miss Grey The masters? They didn't tell. They never told. That's why I've had to force it out of you.
Miles It must have been too bad.
Miss Grey Too bad? What do you mean?
Miles The things I must have said. Too bad for the masters to write down in a letter home.
Miss Grey Nonsense! Those stupid men! It was their duty to write them down. One word of explanation and we'd have known what we were

dealing with. We wouldn't have been in the dark all this time. Well, what were these things you said, Miles, and who taught you them?

Miles (*holding his head again*) I'm sorry, I don't know.

Miss Grey Don't know?

Miles I can't remember.

Miss Grey Miles, you can. Come, the truth can only save you.

Miles I don't know.

Miss Grey No more lies, Miles, or you're lost.

Miles Please, I'm not well.

Miss Grey Miles, why did you go off today?

Miles I thought I told you. For a stroll.

Miss Grey For eight hours?

Miles I had to think.

Miss Grey Think about what?

Miles About the queer way you bring me up. About Uncle not caring enough to take any interest in me.

Miss Grey Your uncle's an extremely busy man, Miles.

Miles Yes, and my life's passing by.

Miss Grey Nonsense, your life's only just begun. Miles, who did you meet on this stroll?

Miles I've told you. Nobody.

Miss Grey I believe you met somebody and spent the day with them.

Miles I don't know anybody.

Miss Grey I believe you're carrying on a friendship that you try to conceal from me.

Miles What friendship? Who with?

Miss Grey Miles, Miles, you know. When did it all begin?

Miles I don't know what you mean.

Miss Grey Was it as soon as they died?

Pause

Miles Died? Is this a joke?

Miss Grey You're lying again. You're lying. Don't you want to be saved?

Miles Have you heard from your family again?

Miss Grey Don't be impertinent, you little imp of Satan!

He holds his head again

No, Miles, you can't deceive me with your imaginary headaches.

Miles Please. I feel rotten. Let me out.

He starts for the window, but she stops him

Miss Grey No. You don't leave this room until I have the truth, even if we're here for a hundred years.

Miles Miss Grey, you're frightening me.

Miss Grey Me, frightening you? But I'm protecting you, don't you see? There are demons all around us.

Miles No!

Miss Grey Yes, and I'm fighting them for your human soul.

Miles No! Keep away! Mrs Grose! I want Mrs Grose!

Miss Grey Mrs Grose has gone. You've got nobody but me, and I've got you. So you're going to tell me everything.

Miles Will you tell me about Bertie the donkey? Tell me about Mrs Lavender.

Miss Grey Miles, when did this all begin?

Miles Nothing began!

Miss Grey Was it the moment they were nailed in their coffins?

Miles Mrs Grose! I want Mrs Grose!

Miss Grey Why do they want you in their power, Miles? What do you do together?

Miles I don't do anything. I want Mrs Grose.

Miss Grey And I want the truth. It's because they were kind to you in their lifetimes, isn't it? They loved you and petted you while your uncle didn't care a jot. You were so hungry for love that you were happy even to welcome souls in torment back from the grave.

Miles No!

Miss Grey You were willing to share in all their horrors and obscenities so long as you could cling to their affection. Am I right?

Miles No! No!

Quint appears at the window

Miss Grey springs forward with a cry to keep Miles with his back to the apparition

Miss Grey Miles, stay as you are! Don't look behind.

Miles What is it? Is it her?

Miss Grey Her? Who do you mean?

Miles Miss Jessel! Miss Jessel!

Miss Grey And why should it be Miss Jessel?

Miles Because that's what you told Flora! That's what made her ill! Is she here?

Miss Grey No, it isn't Miss Jessel. But it's at the window. It's right behind you and it's horrible.

Miles You mean it's him?

Miss Grey Him? Who do you mean by him?

Miles (*looking around wildly*) Peter Quint! Peter Quint, you devil! Where is he? Where?

Miss Grey It doesn't matter, Miles. It doesn't matter, because we've won! He'll never matter any more because I've got you and he's lost you for ever. (*Pointing*) There—there!

Miles breaks from her and faces the window

Miles Where is he? Where?

Miss Grey There. Straight in front of you.

Miles Nothing. There's nothing.

Miss Grey He's there. Look at his white face of damnation. He wants you, Miles, but he won't have you. Never, never, never!

Miles Oh, you devil, you devil! (*He staggers and falls into her arms*)

Quint vanishes

Miss Grey (*holding him*) Miles? Miles! (*She lowers him to the ground and kneels beside him*) Oh, Miles, Miles, you lovely boy, what have we all done to you? (*She stands and steps back*)

Quint appears at the window

Miss Grey shields her face and steps further back. The window swings open and Quint takes a step forward into the room, then turns slowly to extend an inviting hand to someone below in the garden

Miss Jessel glides up from the garden leading Miles, as a ghost, by the hand. His face is as white and grinning as theirs

All three smile at Miss Grey, as the Lights fade to a Black-out

CURTAIN

FURNITURE AND PROPERTY LIST

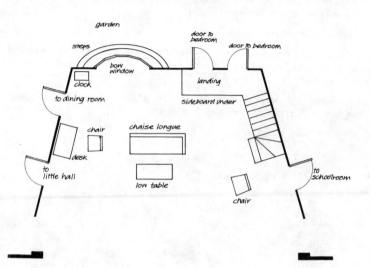

ACT I

On stage: Chaise-longue
Chair
Desk. *In bottom drawer:* rusty key, matches. *On top:* oil lamp
Desk chair
Sideboard
Low table. *On it:* vase
Grandfather clock
Window curtains (open)
Bell-rope
Carpet

PROLOGUE

No properties required

SCENE 1

Personal: **Crimond:** pocket-watch, sealed envelope

SCENE 2

Set: Letter, framed photograph, writing-paper, pen, ink on desk
Off stage: Bunch of flowers **(Flora)**
Basket of flowers **(Miss Grey)**
Bowl of flowers **(Mrs Grose)**

SCENE 3

Strike: Flower-basket, bowl of flowers

Set: Easel, paints, brushes by window
Jigsaw puzzle on low table

Off stage: Letter on salver **(Mrs Grose)**

SCENE 4

Strike: Jigsaw puzzle, easel, paints, brushes, letter

Set: Blanket on *chaise-longue*
Book on floor nearby
Lighted candle on low table
Window curtains closed

Off stage: Lighted candle **(Mrs Grose)**
Tray with two mugs **(Mrs Grose)**

ACT II

SCENE 1

Strike: Blanket, book, tray with mugs

Set: Globe on floor
Knitting (for **Miss Gray**)
Window curtains open

Off stage: Gloves, bible **(Miss Grey)**
Cap **(Miles)**
Bag trailing items of clothing **(Miss Grey)**

SCENE 2

Off stage: Lighted candle **(Mrs Grose)**

SCENE 3

Strike: Globe, knitting, **Miss Grey**'s bag

Set: Key in desk drawer
                Easel, paints, brushes by window
                White sheet, orange, chair by window (for **Mrs Grose**)
                Window curtains open

Off stage: Lighted candle **(Mrs Grose)**

SCENE 4

Strike: Easel, paints, brushes, orange

Set: Chair away from window

Off stage: Tray with plate of food, cutlery, glass, jug of milk **(Miss Grey)**

LIGHTING PLOT

Property fittings required: oil lamp
Interior. A sitting-room/hall. The same scene throughout

ACT I, Prologue.   Night

To open: Pre-dawn gloom with hint of light through window

Cue 1	When ready *Lightning*	(Page 1)
Cue 2	Couple exit through window *Lightning, then fade to Black-out*	(Page 1)

ACT I, Scene 1.   Afternoon

To open: General sunny daylight

Cue 3	**Mrs Grose** curtsies and hurries out *Fade to Black-out*	(Page 8)

ACT I, Scene 2.   Towards dusk

To open: Dim evening light

Cue 4	**Miss Grey** goes back to desk and resumes her letter *Lightning*	(Page 12)
Cue 5	**Miss Grey:** "Then who was it?" *Fade to Black-out*	(Page 14)

ACT I, Scene 3.   Morning

To open: Black-out

Cue 6	When ready *Bring up general daylight*	(Page 14)
Cue 7	**Miss Grey:** "... they're already lost." *Fade to Black-out*	(Page 21)

ACT I, Scene 4.   3 a.m.

To open: Dim lighting; oil lamp lit

Cue 8	**Miss Grey:** "From damnation." *Fade to Black-out*	(Page 27)

ACT II, Scene 1. Afternoon

To open Dull daylight

Cue 9   **Miss Jessel** holds out her arms beseechingly   (Page 34)
             Fade to Black-out

ACT II, Scene 2. Evening

To open: Moonlight through window

Cue 10   **Mrs Grose** lights oil lamp   (Page 34)
             Bring up oil lamp and covering spots

Cue 11   **Mrs Grose** exits; **Miss Grey** picks up pen and thinks   (Page 36)
             Fade to Black-out

ACT II, Scene 3. Late afternoon to evening

To open: Late afternoon light

Cue 12   During scene   (Page 37)
             Gradually fade lighting as evening falls

Cue 13   **Flora** tiptoes upstairs   (Page 40)
             Fade lighting further

Cue 14   **Miss Grey** lights oil lamp   (Page 42)
             Bring up oil lamp and covering spots

Cue 15   **Mrs Grose** starts up the stairs   (Page 45)
             Fade to Black-out

ACT II, Scene 4. Late afternoon

To open: Late afternoon light

Cue 16   **Quint, Miss Jessel** and **Miles** stand smiling at **Miss Grey** (Page 51)
             Fade to Black-out

EFFECTS PLOT

ACT I

Cue 1	When ready *Thunder*	(Page 1)
Cue 2	Couple exit through window *Thunder*	(Page 1)
Cue 3	**Miss Grey:** "... so much good." *Thunder*	(Page 12)
Cue 4	**Miss Grey** starts to mount stairs *Thunder*	(Page 12)
Cue 5	As Scene 3 opens *Piano music, off* L	(Page 14)
Cue 6	Shortly after **Mrs Grose** closes schoolroom door *Cut piano music*	(Page 16)

ACT II

Cue 7	**Miss Grey:** "... your little schemes." *Front door slams, off* R	(Page 33)
Cue 8	**Miss Grey** runs upstairs *Pause, then clock strikes five*	(Page 33)
Cue 9	When ready *Front door opens and closes off* R	(Page 34)
Cue 10	As Scene 3 opens *Piano music off* L	(Page 37)
Cue 11	**Mrs Grose:** "Strange?" *Shortly after cut piano music*	(Page 38)
Cue 12	**Miss Grey:** "... come in here now?" *Flourish on piano off* L	(Page 38)
Cue 13	**Miles** leads **Miss Grey** into schoolroom *Piano music*	(Page 39)
Cue 14	**Miss Grey:** "... hear Miles's song." *Cut piano music*	(Page 40)
Cue 15	**Miles** laughs and begins a wild, incoherent song *Accompanying piano music*	(Page 40)
Cue 16	**Miss Grey:** "Stop that blessed noise!" *Cut piano music*	(Page 40)

MADE AND PRINTED IN GREAT BRITAIN BY
LATIMER TREND & COMPANY LTD PLYMOUTH
MADE IN ENGLAND